New Business Opportunities for EU Companies in Cambodia

An Investor's Guidebook

ASIA INVEST

EUROPEAID
CO-OPERATION OFFICE

C

Consultants and authors of this report:
Mr François CHERER (AETS)
Mr Sarouen CHAK (AETS)
Mrs Marianne DUCAMP (AETS)
ECODES Consortium
Rue de la Loi 26, B-1040 Bruxelles
Tel +32-2-280.17.37 – Fax +32-2-280.19.12

This report has been produced with the assistance of the European Union under the Asia-Invest programme. The views expressed herein are those of the consultant and can therefore in no way be taken to reflect the views of the European Union.

**Europe Direct is a service to help you find answers
to your questions about the European Union**

New freephone number:
00 800 6 7 8 9 10 11

A great deal of additional information on the European Union is available on the Internet.
It can be accessed through the Europa server (http://europa.eu.int).

Cataloguing data can be found at the end of this publication.

Luxembourg: Office for Official Publications of the European Communities, 2005

ISBN 92-894-7527-7

Printed in Belgium

PRINTED ON WHITE CHLORINE-FREE PAPER

SUMMARY

ACRONYMS

ACIAR	Australian Centre for International Agricultural Research
ADB	Asian Development Bank
ADRA	Adventist Development Relief Agency
AFD	Agence Française de Développement (French Development Agency)
AFTA	ASEAN Free Trade Area
APIP	Agricultural Productivity Improvement Project
APSARA	Autorité pour la Protection du Site et l'Aménagement de la Région d'Angkor
AQIP	Agricultural Quality Improvement Project
ASDP	Agricultural Sector Development Project
ASEAN	Association of South East Asian Nations
AVRDC	Asian Vegetable Research and Development Centre
BAT	British American Tobacco
BIT	Bilateral Investment Treaty
BLDP	Buddhist Democratic Party
BOT	Build-Operate-Transfer
CAAEP	Cambodia Australia Agricultural Extension Project
CAMFEBA	Cambodian Federation of employers and Business associations
CARDI	Cambodian Agricultural Research and Development Centre
CDC	Council for the Development of Cambodia
CGIAR	Consultative Group for International Agricultural Research
CIB	Cambodian Investment Board
CIRAD	Centre de Coopération Internationale en Recherche pour le Développement
CPP	Cambodian People's Party
CRC	Conditional registration Certificate
CRDB	Cambodian rehabilitation an Development board
DAALI	Department of Agronomy and Land Improvement
DAE	Department of Agricultural Extension
DFID	Department for International Development (UK)
DREE	Direction des Relations Economiques Extérieures (French Department of External Economic Relations)
EAC	Electricity Authority of Cambodia
EC	European Commission
EdC	Electricité du Cambodge (Cambodian Power Company)
EU	European Union
EurepGAP	European Good Agricultural Practice
FAO	Food and Agriculture Organisation
FDI	Foreign Direct Investment
FRC	Final Registration certificate
FUNCINPEC	Front uni national pour un Cambodge indépendant, neutre, pacifique et coopératif
GAP	Good Agricultural Practice
GATT	General Agreement on Tariffs and Trade
GDP	Gross Domestic Product
GMAC	Garment Manufacturers Association of Cambodia
GMS	Greater Mekong sub-region
GSP	Generalised System of Preference
IFC	International Finance corporation

ILO	International Labor Organisation
IMF	International Monetary Fund
IO	International Organisation
IPM	Integrated Pest Management
IT	Information technology
ITC	International Trade Center
LDC	Least Developed Country
LOI	Law on Investment
MAFF	Ministry of Agriculture, Forestry and Fisheries
MoE&F	Ministry of Economy & Finance
MoFA&IC	Ministry of Foreign Affairs & International Co-operation
MFN	Most Favoured Nation
MIME	Ministry of Industry, Mines and Energy
MOC	Ministry of Commerce
MoEYS	Ministry of Education, Youth and Sports
MOWRAM	Ministry of Water Resources and Meteorology
MPDF	Mekong Private Development Fund
MPTC	Ministry of Post and Telecommunications
MRD	Ministry of Rural Development
MW	Megawatt
MWVA	Ministry of Women's and Veterans' Affairs
NBC	National Bank of Cambodia
NGO	Non Governmental Organisation
NPRS	National poverty reduction strategy
OSB	Overseas Service Bureau
PADAP	Peri-Urban Agriculture Development Project
PDAFF	Provincial Department of Agriculture Forestry and Fisheries
PPA	Power Purchase Agreement
PPI	Private sector Participation in Infrastructure
PPPIO	Plant Protection and Phytosanitary Inspection Office
RGC	Royal Government of Cambodia
SARS	Severe Acute Respiratory Syndrome
SEDPII	2nd Socio-Economic and Development Plan 2001-2005
SME	Small and Medium-size Enterprise
SPS	Sanitary and Phytosanitary measures
SRP	Sam Rainsy Party
SUSPER	Sustainable Development of Peri-Urban Agriculture in
TA (Policy)	Technical Adviser (Policy)
TRIPS	Trade Related aspects of Intellectual Property Rights
UK	United Kingdom
UN	United Nations
UNCTAD	United Nations Conference on Trade and Development
UNDP	United Nations Development Programme
UNTAC	United Nations Transitional Authority for Cambodia
UPOV	Union for Protection of Plant Varieties
USA	United States of America
USD	United States Dollar
VAT	Value added Tax
WB	World Bank
WTO	World Trade Organisation

THAILAND

LAOS

104

106

Sisŏphŏn

Slemréab

Stœng Trêng

Bătdâmbâng

14

14

Tonle Sap

Mekong

Pŏuthĭsăt

Kâmpóng
Chhnăng

Krâchéh

Phnum Adral ▲

Kâmpóng
Cham

12

12

Krōng
Kaôh
Kŏng

PHNOM
PENH

VIETNAM

Kâmpôt

Kâmpóng
Saôm

Gulf of
Thailand

South China
Sea

10

10

106

| 0 | 50 | 100 km |
| 0 | 50 | 100 ml |

Source: Council for Development of Cambodia

INTRODUCTION

This Guidebook for European Investors in Cambodia has been prepared under contract for the European Commission with funding for both the research and production of the Guidebook financed by the Asia-Invest Programme of the EuropeAid Cooperation Office.

This Guidebook and the research behind it are the work of ECODES CONSORTIUM. In the course of their research, the consultants had discussions in many key business centres of the EU Member States and Cambodia in order to validate current financial and factual information, and to gain an insight into the perceptions, motivations and experiences surrounding European investment in Cambodia from both viewpoints.

The Guidebook attempts to deal with the various topics that are likely to be relevant to potential investors and also includes useful internet addresses in order to allow investors to update their information.

The material in this Guidebook is solely provided for the guidance of those contemplating investment, but it is no substitute for professional advice, which should be sought before taking any specific action. The information in this document is believed to be correct as of November 2004 but no responsibility is taken for its accuracy.

This report has been produced with the assistance of the European Union under the Asia-Invest programme. The views expressed herein are those of the consultant and can therefore in no way be taken to reflect the views of the European Union.

The Asia-Invest Programme is an initiative of the European Commission to promote and support business co-operation between the EU and Asia. The Programme provides assistance to business organisations to facilitate mutually beneficial partnerships between companies, in particular small and medium-sized enterprises (SMEs), in the EU and South and South-East Asia and China; as well as to strengthen the business environment to increase trade and investment flows between the two regions.

For further information on the Asia-Invest Programme, please contact:

Asia-Invest Programme

European Commission
EuropeAid Co-operation Office
B-1049 Brussels, Belgium
Tel: +32 (2) 298 4873
Fax: +32 (2) 296 5833
Email: **europeaid-asia-invest@cec.eu.int**
Web site: **www.europa.eu.int/comm/europeaid/projects/asia-invest**

The Delegation of the European Commission to the Kingdom of Cambodia

Nr 1, Street 21,
Tonle Bassac, Chamcarmon
Phnom Penh PO BOX 2301
Cambodia
Tel: +855 (0) 23 216996
Fax: +855 (0) 23 216997
Email: **mailto@delkhm.cec.eu.int**
Web site: **www.delkhm.cec.eu.int**

EXECUTIVE SUMMARY

GENERAL OVERVIEW

Geography

The Kingdom of Cambodia occupies an area of 181 035 square kilometres at the south-western part of the Indochina peninsula. It has boundaries to Thailand, Laos and Vietnam and to the Gulf of Thailand. The most important cities are the capital Phnom Penh with more than 1 million inhabitants, Battambang, Kampong Cham, Siem Reap and Sihanoukville.

Demography

Cambodia's population was estimated at 12.5 million in 2002. It is growing at a rate of 2.25%. The population is very young with 40% of the total below 15 years of age. The average life expectancy is only 58 years. A large proportion of the population (84.3%) live in rural areas. With 73 inhabitants per square kilometre, Cambodia's population density is low compared to other Southeast Asian countries. The Cambodian population is mainly composed of Khmers (around 90%) and several small ethnic minorities including Chinese, Cham and Vietnamese.

Social situation

Cambodia has been devastated by war and isolation in the period between 1975 and 1991. Peace and security have been fully restored since 1998, but Cambodia remains one of the world's "Least Developed Countries" as classified by the United Nations. Cambodia's social situation is characterised by poverty and poor public health and education services, particularly in the rural areas.

Political situation

After the dramatic events of the 1975-1991 period, Cambodia has experienced relative political stability. Following the Paris Peace Accord in 1991 and the intervention of the United Nations Transitional Authority in Cambodia (UNTAC), general elections were held and a new Constitution was promulgated in 1993. Since then, two general elections have been held. Following the last national election (July 2003), a new CPP-FUNCINPEC coalition government was formed (15 July 2004), after a long political stalemate.

Following the abdication of King Norodom Sihanouk, on 14 October 2004, the Throne Council named Norodom Sihamoni as the new King of Cambodia. The coronation ceremony took place on 29 October 2004.

Economic situation

The Cambodian government formed after the 1993 elections formulated comprehensive macroeconomic and structural reforms towards a market-oriented economic system. The objectives set out in the 1994 adjustment and reform programme were to restore economic and financial stability, reform the central institutions of macro-economic management and promote investment for rehabilitation and reconstruction. Current economic policies are set out in the Second Socio-Economic Development Plan 2001-2005 (SEDP II). The Plan aims for macroeconomic stability, targeting an average annual growth rate of 6-7% while maintaining inflation below 4%.

The Plan's objectives of economic growth and poverty reduction recognise the private sector, both domestic and foreign, as an engine of growth and economic development. It also stresses that private sector expansion is dependent on sustained improvements in the governance environment. The Plan sets out the development of the rural economy as a priority to reduce the incidence of poverty. It also stresses the improvement of infrastructure to promote the growth of SMEs and the diversification of exports.

In 2003, the Cambodian government approved the National Poverty Reduction Strategy (NPRS) for 2003-2005, that outlines the policies and programmes required for poverty reduction. In July 2004, the Prime Minister launched the Economic Policy Agenda for the third legislature of the National Assembly, entitled the "Rectangular Strategy" (see page 28).

Overall, economic growth has been strong over the last decade. During the 1999-2002 period the average growth rate was 6.35%. However this has not been sufficient to reduce poverty, with the GDP per capita remaining low at USD 297.

The economic growth experienced has been mainly due to an expanding construction sector and the rapid development of emerging sectors, the garment industry, tourism and telecommunications. By contrast, agriculture, the country's main economic sector employing 77% of the workforce, has remained inefficient and slow growing.

The industrial sector, which was practically non-existent until 1993, has grown at a yearly rate of about 10% since 1995. This has been mostly due to the garment industry, Cambodia's largest industry, employing 230 000 people, which has grown from USD 20 million to USD 1.54 billion in exports from 1995 to 2003.

The services sector has also been growing at a fast rate over the last ten years, mainly due to the expansion of tourism, transportation, trade and telecommunications. Cambodia's tourism sector alone has grown at a yearly rate of 30% over the last two years, the main destination being the unique archaeological sites around Siem Reap, symbolised by the Angkor Wat temple. Telecommunications have also been expanding rapidly since 1996. With the liberalisation of the sector and the advent of private service providers, the mobile phone usage has increased from 23 000 in 1996 to over 320 000 in 2002.

THE BUSINESS ENVIRONMENT

Private sector profile

Cambodia's private sector predominantly consists of small-scale unregistered enterprises involved in agriculture, food processing and services. This informal sector accounts for 80% of GDP and 95% of employment. Registered private enterprises, estimated to number about 10 000, constitute the formal private sector. Almost all companies with foreign direct investment (FDI), the "foreign sector", belong to the formal sector. The foreign sector plays an important role in the Cambodian economy: it is the main source of exports.

With the enactment of the Investment Law in 1994 and due to its privileged access to the US and the EU garment markets, Cambodia has attracted a significant amount of FDI in the years 1996-2003. It has been heavily concentrated in the garment industry, hotels and telecommunications. The main sources of FDI have been Asian countries, primarily Malaysia, Taiwan, China, South Korea and Singapore.

Other investors include a few large US and EU companies and a number of European small and medium-size companies who are mainly involved in the services and construction sectors.

Legal and regulatory framework

In recent years the Cambodian government has made progress in creating an enabling legal framework for the private sector by enacting important laws, such as the Law on Banking and Financial Institutions, the Insurance Law, a new Land Law, the Trademarks Law and the Law on Enterprise Accounting and Auditing. The government has also amended the Investment Law to simplify the investment licensing process and to modify tax incentives offered to qualified investment projects.

Further, the government has drafted new laws that have been pending the resumption of legislative work by parliament. These include the Law on Commercial Enterprises, the Law on Commercial Arbitration, the Commercial Contract Law, the Law on Secured Transactions, the Insolvency Law. The government is also drafting important legislation to establish a commercial court. Several other laws that have a bearing on private sector development are at the drafting stage, such as the Anti-corruption Law, the Law on Customs and the Tourism and Entertainment Law.

In September 2003, the WTO ministerial meeting at Cancun approved Cambodia's accession to the WTO. Cambodia became a member of WTO in October 2004, following the ratification of the accession protocol by the Parliament in September 2004. Cambodia has made a number of commitments relating to its institutions, in particular to step up reforms in its legislative and judicial systems. An ambitious schedule has been set out to enact a total of more than 40 new laws and regulations by 2006 in order to fulfil WTO membership requirements.

Constraints for the private sector

The growth of the private sector in Cambodia over the past ten years has been remarkable. Yet it has been heavily concentrated in a few sectors and areas, and has lacked integration and linkage to the broader economy. The substantial FDI flows seen in the garment, tourism and telecommunications sectors responded to specific opportunities, such as the privileged access to the EU and US markets for garments. In other sectors there has been practically no investment, either domestic or foreign.

The major constraints faced by the private sector are the weak legal, judicial and administrative environment, inadequate physical infrastructure, high costs of doing business, and a limited access to bank financing.

Positive factors

The Cambodian government, with the assistance of international donors, has made progress in reducing some of the physical constraints. Significant improvements are underway in transportation infrastructure, power supply and telecommunications.

The Cambodian work force is reputed to be able and willing. The compliance by Cambodian employers with international social standards set under the Labour Law has been a key element in allowing the Cambodian garment industry to obtain access to the US market.

Cambodia was granted Most Favoured Nation (MFN) status by the EU in 1993, which gave it equally privileged access to EU markets as General Agreement on Tariffs and Trade (GATT) members. Since then, Cambodia has never been subject to quota restrictions by the EU.

In its trade with the EU, Cambodia benefits from the Generalised Scheme of Preferences (GSP) that provides tariff reductions without quantitative limitations. As a "Least Developed Country - LDC" Cambodia is furthermore entitled to benefit from the most favourable treatment under the GSP, the so-called "Everything But Arms – EBA" provisions.

Under the EBA Cambodia is entitled to duty-free and quota-free access to the EU for all its exports, except arms and ammunitions. The EU-Cambodia Textiles Agreement allows Cambodian producers to export garments to the EU based on rules of origin which include the possibility of regional accumulation of origin.

Cambodia is a member of ASEAN, the Association of South-East Asian Nations. The 10 member countries have a population of about 550 million. They constitute a diverse group in terms of economic development and wealth, but they represent one of the world's important trade and investment areas. ASEAN is engaged in an economic integration process, including the ASEAN Free Trade Area (AFTA) currently being implemented and the establishment of the Asian Economic Community (AEC) set as the end-goal of economic integration by the year 2020. An ambitious programme of action towards integration is underway covering trade and investment, including a plan to integrate 11 priority sectors within the ASEAN region.

Cambodia's accession to the WTO will protect its garment industry after the removal of export quotas at the end of 2004 under the Multi-Fibre Agreement (MFA) arrangements, which will be applicable to WTO members. Cambodia will be able to benefit from rights accorded to all members such as non-discrimination by other members (Most Favoured Nation treatment) and access to the dispute settlement procedure. Cambodia will also benefit from the Goods Dispute Settlement Mechanisms.

POTENTIAL FOR EU-CAMBODIA BUSINESS CO-OPERATION

Tourism

Tourism has grown remarkably since 1993, with particular strong growth since 1999 due to improved security and infrastructure. The number of tourist arrivals increased from 368 000 to 786 000 between 1999 and 2002. In 2003, the Iraq war and the SARS epidemic disrupted the industry, resulting in a decrease of arrivals. For 2004, a strong rebound of growth is expected and the upward trend should continue over the coming years. The Siem Reap area alone, where the Angkor temple is located, received about 450 000 foreign visitors in 2002.

Besides restored security and improved infrastructure, several factors have helped in facilitating the arrival of tourists, mainly the "open-skies" policy and the possibility to obtain visas on arrival.

Hospitality facilities have expanded to meet the demand. The number of hotels has increased from 125 in 1993 to 292 (13169 rooms) in 2003. Since 1994, total investment in hotels has amounted to over USD 700 million.

At present, most foreign tourists visit Cambodia as part of a regional tour and only stay for a few days in Siem Reap/Angkor However Cambodia has the potential to become a major destination in its own right. When infrastructure improves, Cambodia's natural resources including the national parks, wild life sanctuaries and the rich eco-system of the Tonle Sap Lake will represent a significant asset in attracting tourists.

The government has drafted a Tourism and Entertainment Law that will constitute the necessary regulatory framework for the expansion of hospitality activities. In particular the law will set quality standards in line with international practice.

Infrastructure and facilities are just adequate to accommodate the current level of visitors to the main destinations of Phnom Penh and Siem Reap/Angkor. The expansion of tourism to other areas will become possible when transportation infrastructure and accommodation facilities are built. At this time another constraint is the scarcity of a skilled workforce and the lack of training facilities.

For EU companies, there are opportunities in the Cambodian tourism sector. They can supply equipment, goods and services to Cambodian operators. They can also provide technical assistance, management services and training courses. EU tour operators can buy and distribute travel products designed and delivered by Cambodian firms. EU investors should also seriously consider the potential offered by Cambodia's unique attractions.

Agro-processing

Cambodia's agricultural GDP is composed of food and industrial crops (50%), fisheries (30%), livestock (14%) and forestry (6%).

Developing its agriculture is essential for Cambodia; it is one of the top priorities of the government and the international development agencies. Although progress has been achieved over the last ten years, such as in the increase of rice production yield from 1,3 to 2,1 tons per hectare, there is great potential for growth in the area of primary production, and furthermore in the area of processing. Agro-industry is only nascent. It accounts for 3,2% of GDP and provides less than 1% of total employment.

All assessments made by the government and donor agencies emphasise the need for agricultural diversification and agri-business. There is unanimous agreement that this represents one of the only ways of developing the country and that potential for successful investments by the private sector is high.

The government's strategy to develop agriculture and agro-industries consists in promoting a consistent macroeconomic and agricultural policy framework; establishing policy and legal frameworks for effective land management and administration; accelerating irrigation development; strengthening agricultural support services and developing quality standards.

The Land Law enacted in 2001 provides the framework for land ownership in the country and provides the legal mechanism for titling and land dispute resolution.

The government is drafting legislation to allow the development of a system of geographical indications in line with the TRIPS Agreement of the WTO. This system will enable Cambodian producers of specialty agricultural products to benefit from this intellectual rights protection and to obtain better prices for their products. In addition, the government is drafting a Water Law to address the problem of insufficient irrigation infrastructure.

The Cambodian agro-industrial sector consists of a large number of small and micro-enterprises with little integration among themselves and with the markets. The majority of the small firms are rice millers. Others process simple food products such as fish paste and sauce, fermented vegetables, baked goods and dried fruit. In Phnom Penh and other main cities, there are a few larger food processing companies, including noodle manufacturers, small canneries, soy and chilli sauce makers and bottling plants. There are only a few sizeable companies in the agro-industrial sector in Cambodia, with hardly any foreign investment, except for a large European company in tobacco processing.

The development of an active agro-industrial sector is hampered by a number of factors, including land ownership issues, inadequate infrastructure, and limited access to quality inputs.

More generally, entrepreneurs in agro-industry are constrained by the lack of capital and limited access to external financial support, lack of information on markets, difficult access to the markets due to insufficient means of transportation and to administrative obstacles, lack of technology and lack of skills.

On the positive side, Cambodia's farmers and food product manufacturers manage to provide consumers with a diverse range of products, which testifies to the traditional ability of the country and its farmers. Being free from polluting industries, Cambodia has a competitive advantage in producing organic agricultural products.

EU companies can contribute to the development of Cambodia's agro-industrial sector by selling equipment, inputs and services and buying Cambodian products (in particular specialty products that will benefit from the legislation on geographical indications, such as pepper, other spices and herbs, varietal rice). As overall conditions improve, there will also be interesting opportunities for EU companies to employ their capital and know-how in agriculture development and agro-industrial projects in Cambodia. The improved enforcement of land concessions, in particular, will be an essential element that will allow investment in large integrated operations.

Infrastructure

Cambodia's low income, low population density and recent history are reflected in the poor coverage, quality and efficiency of much of its infrastructure. The existing services are concentrated in the urban areas; the rural majority of the population has little access to adequate roads or other transportation means, reliable supply of electricity and safe water, and telephone connections.

Unlike most developing countries, Cambodia has acquired a significant experience in private sector participation in infrastructure (PPI). Foreign investors are involved in telecommunications and airports and a sizeable number of Cambodian entrepreneurs own and operate small power and water networks.

The participation of the private sector in a number of projects has been a positive development for Cambodia, and the government intends to expand the involvement of local and foreign investors in infrastructure projects. However the practice of PPI will need to improve substantially to achieve standards that will be conducive to sustained interest on the part of foreign investors.

The legal and regulatory framework for PPI projects in Cambodia is still at an early stage of formulation and implementation. This is also true of the institutional and procedural framework. An overall law on PPI is at the drafting stage, it will take some time before it is finalised. In some sectors, like the power sector, legislation has been completed and subsequent organisational and institutional changes have been implemented. In the other sectors, laws are being drafted and institutions have not yet changed.

The sectors of power, telecommunications and water are the main sectors where private sector participation appears to have good potential.

In the power sector, the 2001 Electricity Law has clarified the institutional roles, with the Ministry of Industry, Mines and Energy (MIME) as policy-maker, the Electricity Authority of Cambodia (EAC) performing the regulatory function and the Cambodian Power Company (EdC) and other operators actually producing and distributing electricity.

Cambodia's electricity sector is expected to grow substantially over the coming years. EdC alone will not be able to meet the requirements due to its insufficient investment capacity; therefore there will be opportunities for private operators and investors to get involved in this market.

Opportunities for EU companies will be in providing equipment and services, and in investing in projects initiated by Cambodian authorities or by private investors.

Unlike in the power sector, the legal and regulatory framework for the telecommunications sector has not yet been modernised, although a new Telecommunications Law has been under preparation for some time. The new law would create a telecommunication regulatory authority, under the Ministry of Post and Telecommunications, which would regulate the sector and grant licenses to operators.

The Cambodian telecommunications sector is growing rapidly. Mobile phone services in particular have experienced a very fast growth due to the inadequate coverage of fixed line networks.

EU companies can take advantage of opportunities offered by this fast growing sector by providing equipment and services and by investing in new projects.

The water sector is ruled by a loose set of legislations, the main ones being the 1996 Law on the General Status of Public Enterprises, based on which the Phnom Penh Water Supply Authority (PPWSA) was established. According to the government's strategy the supply of water should meet local requirements, service provision should be decentralised, an independent regulator should be set up and private sector participation should be encouraged.

With the expected expansion of the water networks in Phnom Penh and the main provincial cities, there will be opportunities for EU firms to compete in this market.

In terms of investment, there may be some immediate opportunities for the EU companies that are specialised in installation and managing water supply facilities and networks. In the longer term, there may be openings by way of participation in the possible privatisation of the larger water utilities such as the PPWSA.

PART I

Cambodia overview

1. Recent history

Independence 1953 -1969

Before 1953, Cambodia was under French protectorate for almost a century. The independence from France was won by King Norodom Sihanouk on 9 November 1953 after a struggle started in 1945. In 1947 Cambodia's first French-inspired constitution had been promulgated, giving most of the powers to the National Assembly. After a period of conflicts between the government and the King, he not only succeeded in obtaining independence from France but in 1954 he defeated a Vietminh intervention in the north-east of Cambodia. The subsequent Geneva Conference (July 1954) that sanctioned the withdrawal of Vietnamese troops was a victory for Cambodia and a personal triumph for the King.

Sangkum Reastr Niyum

In 1955 the King decided to abdicate in favour of his father, Norodom Suranmarit, and he founded a political alliance by the name of Sangkum Reastr Niyum, that won the elections. From 1955 to the end of 1969, Cambodia enjoyed economic growth and security. It produced rice surpluses, constructed infrastructure including the Sihanoukville port, roads, railways, power plants and established industries. An urban middle class started to emerge, whose income became much higher than the rural population and the poor urban workers.

The Khmer Republic 1970-1975

In the late 1960's the leadership of Prince Sihanouk faltered and economic progress lagged. The social cohesion of the Cambodian people started to erode.

On the international front, the Prince's balancing act between the western powers, the USSR and China, and the relations with Vietnam became untenable. After a troubled period, Prince Sihanouk was ousted from power on 18 March 1970, while he was in France, by a coup staged by general Lon Nol and Prince Sisowath Sirik Matak.

The new regime called the Khmer Republic was installed on 9 October 1970. General Lon Nol assumed the position of President. After being forced from power, Prince Sihanouk settled in Beijing and mobilised forces to fight against the American-supported Lon Nol government. Communist forces in Cambodia, which had emerged in the late 1960s, joined Prince Sihanouk to form the National United Front of Kampuchea with the support of North Vietnam. This initiated Cambodia's civil war.

Democratic Kampuchea 1975-1979

With a deteriorating economy, insecurity and the destruction of large areas of the countryside by the US bombings, the country plunged into instability and Lon Nol was desta-bilised despite his attempts to create a new regime with a new constitution. Following riots, a growing number of people, including students left Phnom Penh to join the Khmer Rouges who had been building armed forces for several years.

After several attacks against provincial towns, the Khmer Rouges captured Phnom Penh on 17 April 1975. They established a regime called Democratic Kampuchea, under the leadership of Pol Pot. The regime implemented a Maoist communist system based on ultra-collectivism, with the objective of eradicating the old order represented by city people and the Buddhist religion. Market economy and business activities were completely abolished, private ownership was forbidden. The entire urban population was forced to leave the cities and to work in the fields. An estimated 1.2 million people were massacred or died from starvation or disease. The regime destroyed Cambodian society and left the country in a political, economic and social vacuum.

The People's Republic of Kampuchea 1979-1990

On 7 January 1979, Vietnamese troops and Cambodian resistance forces entered into Cambodia and drove the Pol Pot regime out of Phnom Penh. Khmer Rouge forces withdrew to the Thai-Cambodian border areas and continued the civil war. A new government was established under the name of People's Republic of Kampuchea (PRK). The PRK, headed by Heng Samrin, was supported by Vietnam and the USSR while the Western powers, China and ASEAN countries supported the Khmer Rouge and the non-communist resistant forces fighting against the PRK.

The Heng Samrin regime was controlled by the communist party, first called the People's Revolutionary Party of Cambodia, then the Cambodian People's Party (CPP). The Vietnamese socialist system was the model. The state performed all foreign trade, owning and operating all enterprises. Development efforts were initiated based on collectivism. With such policies, and with civil war continuing, Cambodia's economy was devastated, with most people living in poverty. The government's budget depended heavily on assistance from the socialist bloc.

The State of Cambodia and the UNTAC; The Kingdom of Cambodia 1991-1998

In 1987, the reconciliation process began between Norodom Sihanouk and then Prime Minister Hun Sen. Two years later, the final contingent of Vietnamese troops left Cambodia. The PRK was renamed the State of Cambodia. On 23 October 1991, the four main political factions signed the Peace accords in Paris and in March 1992 the United Nations Transitional Authority in Cambodia (UNTAC) arrived in Cambodia to assist in governing the country until elections could be held.

Following difficulties in restoring peace and security, caused by the continuing fighting by the Khmer Rouge faction and the repatriation of 360 000 refugees, the UNTAC succeeded in organising general elections in May 1993. A coalition government was formed among the three main political parties: FUNCINPEC, CPP and BLDP.

With a new constitution promulgated, the State of Cambodia became the Kingdom of Cambodia and Norodom Sihanouk was reinstated as King. The constitution established a liberal democratic state with a market economy.

In 1997 serious political tensions emerged within the coalition government which erupted into fighting between different factions of the armed forces in Phnom Penh. This caused the economy to slump and foreign aid agencies and investors to leave the country. In late 1997, political parties resumed negotiations and reached an agreement to hold elections that took place in July 1998. The three parties, CPP, FUNCINPEC and SRP (Sam Rainsy Party), gained seats in the National Assembly and a new coalition government was formed between CPP and FUNCINPEC in November 1998.

Mass defections of Khmer Rouge soldiers and the death of Pol Pot in early 1998 ended three decades of civil war.

Relative stability and progress 1998 -2004

In accordance with the constitution, general elections were subsequently held in July 2003. The CPP won a majority of seats, but it did not reach the 75% majority that would have allowed it to form a government. Following a long political stalemate that brought the country's legislative and executive action to a standstill, a CPP-FUNCINPEC coalition government was formed on 15 July 2004.

Following the abdication of King Norodom Sihanouk, on 14 October 2004, the Throne Council named Norodom Sihamoni as the new King of Cambodia. The coronation ceremony took place on 29 October 2004.

2. Geography and climate

Cambodia is a small country, bordered by three neighbours: Thailand and the Lao People's Democratic Republic in the west and north, the Socialist Republic of Viet Nam in the east and southeast, and the sea, the Gulf of Thailand in the southwest.

The country occupies an area of 181 035 square kilometres. This is around twice the size of Portugal. According to official figures of the Ministry of Agriculture, Forestry and Fisheries (CMDG report, MAFF 2003), 61% of the country's total area is covered by forest and 20% is agricultural land.

The dominant features of the Cambodian landscape are lowland regions consisting of plains around the Tonle Sap Lake, the Tonle Sap River, and the Mekong and Bassac river systems. Surrounding these central plains, which cover three quarters of the area, are the more densely forested and sparsely populated highlands: the Elephant mountains and Cardamom mountains of the southwest and west regions; the Dangrek mountains of the north, adjoining the Korat plateau of Thailand; and the Ratanakiri plateau and Chlong highland on the east, merging with the central highlands of Viet Nam.

The climate is a tropical monsoon climate with two main seasons: a warm and rainy monsoon season from May to November and a dry season from December to April. The average temperature is around 27°C.

3. Demography[1]

The population was around 12.5 million in 2002 (varying according to several sources), with an annual growth rate of 2.5%. The population is very young with 40% of the total below 15 years of age and a proportion of females above the usual average of 52%.

The life expectancy is very low compared to developed countries, only 58 years for the total population (Male: 55.49 years; Female: 60.47 years).

Cambodia is mainly composed of Khmers (around 90%) and other small ethnic minorities including Chinese, Cham and others.

Buddhism is recognised by the Constitution as the national religion: 90% of the population is Buddhist. Other religions like Islam and Christianity are allowed to practise their faiths without any restriction.

A large proportion of the population (84.3%) lives in rural areas.

---

1 Sources: UNCTAD (World Bank 2002); IMF 2003 Fund staff estimates on data provided by Cambodian authorities

4. Politics and government

After the conclusion of the Paris Peace Accord in 1991, the completion of the United Nations Transitional Authority in Cambodia's (UNTAC) mandate and the general elections in 1993, a new Constitution was promulgated on 24 September 1993. The Constitution was amended in March 1999 to establish the Senate.

4.1 Constitution

Liberal Democracy and Monarchy

The Constitution is defined as the supreme law of the Kingdom of Cambodia. All laws and decisions by public institutions must strictly conform to its provisions. The Constitution declares liberal democracy and a multiparty system as the foundations of the political regime of the Kingdom of Cambodia. It declares a market economy as the foundation of Cambodia's economic system. The Constitution provides for the role of the Monarchy, the King being the Head of State for life, who reigns as a symbol of unity and the eternity of Cambodia, but does not govern. The Cambodian people exercise their powers through the National assembly, the Senate, the Royal Government and the Judiciary. The Legislative, Executive and Judicial branches of government are separate.

The National Assembly holds primary legislative power. Decisions on draft laws are made by a single majority of the entire Assembly membership. Today, the National Assembly consists of 123 members elected through national elections to serve five-year terms.

The Senate is the second legislative body. Its role is to review draft laws approved by the National Assembly or other issues submitted by the National Assembly for examination. The Senate currently consists of 61 members who are either appointed or elected in a "non-universal election" to serve six-year terms.

The Royal Government of Cambodia ("RGC") is formed by a vote of confidence by a two-thirds majority of the National Assembly. It is in charge of overall execution of national policies and programmes, and is accountable to the National Assembly. The Government is led by a prime minister, assisted by deputy prime ministers, senior ministers, ministers and secretaries of state.

Since 1993, two general elections have been held. On 15 July 2004 a new CPP-FUNCINPEC coalition government was formed.

An important thrust of government policy has been towards decentralisation. In February 2002, local elections at the commune level were held for the first time and 11 261 councillors were elected to 1 621 commune councils. Similarly a programme of "devolution" of public service delivery has been initiated. A number of Ministries have begun to assess the potential service delivery role for commune councils.

4.2 Foreign policy

The Constitution sets out Cambodia's policies of permanent neutrality, nonalignment and peaceful coexistence with other countries. It prohibits engagement in any military alliance and does not permit the establishment of foreign military bases on Cambodian territory.

Cambodia is a full member of the international community, of the United Nations and other main international institutions. It became a member of the Association of South-East Asian Nations (ASEAN) in April 1999. At the Cancun Conference in September 2003, Cambodia was the first "Least Developed Country" to have concluded negotiations to become a member of the WTO. Cambodia has signed Bilateral Investment Treaties with 15 countries and organisations, including with France, Germany and the Netherlands.

Only a relatively small number of countries maintain permanent embassies in Cambodia. Among EU countries, France, Germany, Poland and the UK have embassies. Most other EU Member States have diplomatic representations in nearby Bangkok. The European Commission established a permanent Delegation in Phnom Penh in 2002.

4.3 Human resources, education and vocational training

Cambodia's human resource base has been devastated by two decades of war and isolation. It is today affected by the low level of public expenditure on education, which stood at a mere 1.85 % of GDP in 2002. The under-re sourcing of the education sector has increased reliance on households and donor contributions, 46% of education expenditures being provided by donors against 27% contributed by the state budget, according to a recent report by the World Bank.

Primary and secondary schooling

In spite of these constraints, Cambodia has improved access to primary and secondary schooling during the past ten years. A nine-year basic education has been introduced. This has resulted to an increase in the youth literacy rate (15-24 years) has increased from 69.9% in 1985 to 75% in 1998, according to data from the Population Census.

The government education reform strategy is embedded in the Education Strategic Plan and the Education Sector Support

Program 2001-2005 (ESSP). A number of donors, including the EC, ADB, World Bank, UNICEF/AIDS, France, Japan and Sweden are contributing to support the ESSP. Its first six-year phase is expected to cost USD 725 million, of which the government will contribute two-thirds and donors one-third. The government's objective is to bring enrolment rates for primary education to 90% and for lower secondary education to 50% by 2005.

Higher education

The higher education system comprises five public universities, three semi-independent specialised institutes and six private higher education institutions.

Participation in higher education is low. Total enrolment was 23 000 in 1999, a rate of 204 per 100 000 people. There has been a trend in favour of private institutions following the establishment of a private university in 1997. This phenomenon is concentrated in Phnom Penh. MoEYS reports the presence of 9 Public Tertiary Institutions and 18 Private Tertiary Institutions.

Vocational training

One of the priorities of the SEDP is to develop technical and vocational skills. The government has devised a National Vocational Training Strategy with the assistance of the ADB and other aid agencies. Private sector and NGO-run programmes constitute more than 80% of current technical vocational education and training[2].

4.4 Health and welfare

The Cambodian health system has developed rapidly from very low levels ten years ago. The Ministry of Health has designed a sector-wide Health Strategic Plan for 2003-2007. It has defined a national health policy that includes major financial reforms and a national system of primary health care coverage. The health system comprises public facilities, which are poorly funded and equipped, and a diverse range of private sector services including clinics and practitioners, which are largely unregulated and of questionable quality. The private sector, including traditional healers and non-qualified drug sellers, is the predominant source of medical care for the majority of the population.

There is no public health insurance in Cambodia and almost no private health insurance, although some employers assist employees with medical expenses. Fees and other expenses at public and private hospitals are high, and represent a real financial burden for people seeking treatment. Some NGOs have designed financing schemes to allow the poor to have access to health care.

---

[2] *Sources:* World Bank2003; http://www.moeys.gov.kh/

5. Economic overview

5.1 Performance since 1993

Performance since 1993

The Cambodian government formed after the 1993 elections formulated comprehensive macroeconomic and structural reform towards a market-oriented economic system with the co-operation and financial assistance of the international community. The objectives set out in the 1994 adjustment and reform programme were to restore economic and financial stability, reform the central institutions of macroeconomic management and promote investment for rehabilitation and reconstruction.

In 1994-1995, economic growth was strong, achieving the government's target of 7 to 8%. It generated substantial employment and revenues. From 1997 to 1998, renewed political tensions combined with the regional financial crisis led to a growth slowdown.

After the formation of a new coalition government in 1998, Cambodia again experienced a period of strong, non-inflationary growth.

	1999	2000	2001	2002	2003 Estimation
Real GDP rates	6.9%	7.7%	6.3%	4.5%	.5.2

Source: IMF 4/02/2003 CAMBODIA report for 1999-2001, based on NIS data and Euro stat; DG Trade for 2002 and World Bank estimates 2003.

This growth was mainly the result of an expanding construction sector and rapid development of emerging sectors: the garment industry, tourism and telecommunications.

5.2 Economic structure

GDP by sectors: Agriculture, Industry, Services

5.3 Agriculture

Agriculture is Cambodia's main economic sector, employing 77% of the work force and representing 32% of GDP in 2001. However, it is a slow growing (average growth of 2.6% between 1993 and 2000) and inefficient sector. The agricultural GDP is made of food and industrial crops for 50-53%, fisheries for 30-32%, livestock for 14-15% and forestry 6%. Rice is the staple food, for which self-sufficiency was achieved in 1995/1996. The Agricultural Development Plan for the period 2001-2005 sets out an increase in rice production from 3,8 million tons in 2000/2001 to 4,8 million tons in 2005/2006 through an increase of the cultivated area from 2175 million ha to 2.5 million ha and an increase in yield from 1.87 ton/ha to 2.0 ton /ha.

Other crops include maize, vegetables, soybean and cassava. Industrial crops include rubber, tobacco and some jute.

Cambodia
Agriculture
in 1000 Tons

	1997	1998	1999	2000	2001	2002	2003
Agriculture							
Rice	3 415	3 510	4 040	4 026	4 099	3 823	4 710
Maize	42	49	95	183	186	266	601
Casava	77	67	228	145	142	122	330
Sweet potato	29	30	32	35	26	32	35
Vegetables	250	217	182	166	185	143	140
Mung bean	15	9	16	15	17	23	32
Peanut	7	7	9	7	7	10	18
Soybean	56	28	35	28	28	39	63
Sesame	7	5	7	10	10	10	22
Sugar cane	188	133	160	213	169	209	173
Tobacco	10	10	6	6	5	3	8
Jute	2	1	"	"	"	1	1
Rubber	32	34	45	42	38	33	33

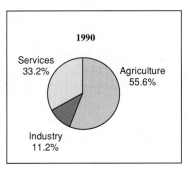

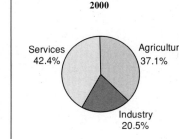

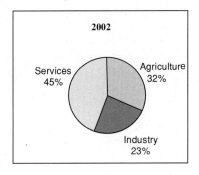

Source: EU- DG Trade, June 2003.

Livestock							
Cattle	2 872	2 680	2 826	3 490	3 495	2 924	2 985
Buffalo	766	694	654	"	626	626	660
Pig	2 237	2 339	2 189	1 979	2 114	2 105	2 304
Poultry	11 982	13 167	13 417	15 028	15 248	16 677	16 013
Fisheries							
Fresh fish & shrimp	115	122	124	86	191	360	390
Crocodiles (heads)	17	41	25	26	36	50	78

Source: Ministry of planning- National institute of statistic (NIS).

During 2002 the agricultural sector experienced a serious setback mainly due to climatic conditions that caused floods and drought. Rice production dropped to 3.7 million tons, down from 4.1 million tons in 2001. Altogether the production of crops declined by 7% in 2002.

The output of fisheries also declined (-13%), as well as the production of rubber and forestry products. In contrast, production of livestock and poultry rose by 8%.

The overall poor performance of agricultural production resulted in the sector only contributing 29% of GDP in 2002.

This underscored the urgency of structural reforms that are being addressed by the Government and international donors.

5.4 Industry

Industry, which was practically non-existent until 1993 except for a small state-owned manufacturing sector, has been growing at a yearly rate of about 10% since 1995.

It contributed 25% of GDP and employed about 8% of the labour force in 2001. This impressive performance has been mostly due to the export-oriented garment industry. Other sectors like the food and tobacco industries progressed slowly in line with the population growth as these industries exclusively cater Cambodia's internal market. Activities in the timber sector declined sharply as a result of the policies against illegal logging. The construction sector, representing about 20% of industrial activities, has been progressing well with renewed confidence in the private sector and increased public investment in infrastructure.

Most of the factories are located in or around Phnom Penh. Other production facilities are located near the Sihanoukville port in an area that is set to become an Export Processing Zone (EPZ). There are also plans to establish similar EPZs on areas bordering Thailand, such as Koh Kong and Poipet.

5.4.1 The garment industry: main sector of national industry

The garment industry is Cambodia's largest industry, with more than 200 factories employing around 250000 people, mostly in Phnom Penh and its suburbs. Within nine years,

from 1995 to 2003, it has grown from USD 20 million to USD 1.54 billion in exports, primarily to the USA and the EU. About 75% of exports consist in woven garments, single transformation stage products with little value addition, the balance being knitwear garments in which value added is higher.

The industry was developed by foreign investors, mostly from neighbouring Asian countries, who usually operate similar garment assembly units in other Asian countries or elsewhere in the world. The main impetus for their move to Cambodia was the privileged market access to the USA and the EU. The industry is totally dependent on imported materials, accessories and other inputs. So far, little attempt has been made to increase the local components used in the garments, and local entrepreneurs have not invested in backward linkage activities, but the Cambodian government is proactively trying to attract FDI in this area.

Besides market access, the industry's strengths are competitive wages (even though wages in Cambodia are not the lowest in Asia), a reputation for consistent quality and the compliance with social norms. In collaboration with ILO, the Cambodian government and the industry have put in place a system to monitor the respect of core labour standards that have resulted in increased quotas from the USA, based on the provisions of the US-Cambodia Bilateral Textile Agreement.

The industry's weaknesses are the low added value of the bulk of the products, the lack of a national supply chain and the difficulties it faces in reducing delivery lead times due to Cambodia's inadequate infrastructure and its weak export administration, with corruption and inadequate trade procedures being cited as key problems. The government is aware of these problems and is promoting investment in the textile industry so as to establish important elements of the supply chain in Cambodia. Dyeing and finishing plants would be key elements in this chain. Potential investors could be textile operators in high cost countries like the EU, who would transfer their plants to Cambodia.

The dramatic change in market environment due to take place on 1 January 2005 with the removal of Multi-Fibre Agreement (MFA) quotas will create a new situation for Cambodia's garment industry. Cambodia will have to face stiffer competition vis-à-vis countries with integrated textile industries and more competitive business conditions. The Cambodian government and the industry will place emphasis on social norms compliance to maintain Cambodia's market share. It remains to be seen whether this strategy will be effective in maintaining buyers' orders at their present level. The RGC is also implementing a comprehensive programme of customs' reform that should result in the improvement of the business environment, with a reduction of both official and unofficial costs and delivery-times.

5.4.2 Salary comparisons in Asia

Here under is shown a comparison of salaries in the garment industry in Asia, which is one of the main comparative indicator in terms of labour rate.

SALARY IN THE CAMBODIAN GARMENT SECTOR IN COMPARISON WITH OTHER COUNTRIES IN THE REGION

Country	Wage (per month)	Year
Bangladesh	40	1996
Indonesia	40	1999
India	57	1999
Vietnam	60	2000
Cambodia	**61**	**2000**
Sri Lanka	63	1998
Thailand	106	1999
Philippines	182	1999
China	191	1997
Malaysia	296	1995

Source: US Department of Labor and Bureau of International Labor Affairs.

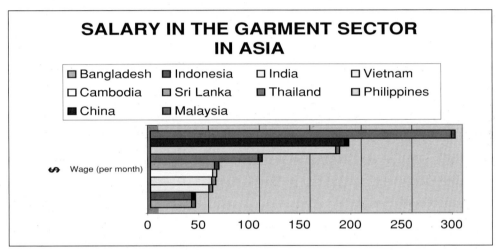

Source: US Department of Labor and Bureau of International Labor Affairs.

5.5 Services

The services sector, which represents about 45% of GDP, has also been growing at a fast rate over the last ten years, mainly due to the expansion of tourism, transportation, trade and telecommunications. Cambodia's tourism sector alone has grown at a yearly rate of 30% over the last two years, the main destination being the unique archaeological sites around Siem Reap, symbolised by the Angkor Wat temple.

Telecommunications have also been expanding rapidly since 1996. With the liberalisation of the sector and the advent of private service providers, the mobile phone usage has increased from 23 000 in 1996 to over 650 000 in 2003.

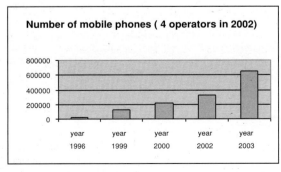

Source: DREE- Phnom Penh.

5.6 Natural resources

Oil and Gas

Offshore exploration by international consortia has produced findings with estimates of gas reserves of about 5 billion cubic metres in Cambodian waters alone. In the areas that are disputed by Cambodia and Thailand, for which an agreement in principle to share the output on a 50-50 basis has been concluded between the two countries, gas reserves of 8 billion cubic metres have been estimated.

Initial studies have also been carried out onshore, in the Tonle Sap area, with encouraging results.

Mineral resources

Mining potential exists in respect of phosphates, limestone, bauxite, copper and zinc manganese. Exploration of gold has started on two sites and there is also potential in gemstones mining and some iron ore.

Hydropower potential

There is substantial hydropower capability in Cambodia that has been estimated at over 8 000 MW, about 50% of which from the Mekong river.

5.7 Cambodia's internal market

Cambodia has a relatively small population of 12.5 million people and GDP per capita stood at USD 297 in 2003. There is however an urban middle class, concentrated in Phnom Penh and other main cities such as Siem Reap, that has sufficient purchasing power to buy durable consumer goods and other consumer items. It is estimated that this could represent a market of about 1.2 million people with an average yearly revenue of about USD 1 300. There is also an estimated 200 000 people with higher revenues that would be equivalent to the income of average Europeans.

5.8 Economic reforms and policies

Economic policies are embedded in the Socio-Economic Development Plan (SEDP).

SEDP II

Current economic policies and a strategic vision for economic growth and poverty reduction are set out in the Second Socio-Economic Development Plan 2001-2005 (SEDP II).

Its main objectives are:

- economic growth to reduce poverty
- development of the private sector
- good governance

SEDP II's strategy for poverty reduction aims at macroeconomic stability, targeting an average annual growth rate of 6 to 7% while maintaining inflation below 4%. The fiscal strategy is aimed at improving revenue mobilisation by improving tax collection and addressing the problem of smuggling.

SEDP II also intends to improve fiscal transparency and carry out public administration reform by increasing civil service pay and introducing anti-corruption legislation. It provides a strategic vision for economic growth and poverty reduction by recognising the private sector, both domestic and foreign, as an engine of growth and economic development. It also stresses that private sector expansion is largely dependent on sustained improvements in the governance environment.

SEDP II sets out the development of the rural economy as a priority to reduce the incidence of poverty. It also stresses the improvement of infrastructure to promote the growth of small and medium-sized enterprises (SMEs) and the diversification of exports.

National Poverty Reduction Strategy (NPRS)

In 2003, the Cambodian government approved the National Poverty Reduction Strategy (NPRS) for 2003-2005. It outlines the policies and programmes required for poverty reduction in order to achieve the targets set out in SEDP II. It sets government revenues targets reaching 14% of GDP by 2005, a significant increase from the 1998 level of 9%.

The Rectangular Strategy

In July 2004, The Prime Minister launched the economic policy agenda of the Cambodian government for the third legislature, entitled the "Rectangular Strategy". The core of the Rectangular Strategy is good governance focused on areas of four reform: anti-corruption, legal and judicial reform, public administration reform and reform of the armed forces.

The environment for the implementation of the strategy consists of four elements: peace, political stability and social order; partnership in development with all stakeholders; favourable macroeconomic and financial environment and integration of Cambodia into the region and the world.

The four strategic "growth triangles" are: enhancement of the agricultural sector; private sector growth and employment; continued rehabilitation and construction of physical infrastructure and capacity building and human resource development.

Financial Sector Blueprint

The Financial Sector Blueprint for 2001-2010 was developed and adopted by the Cambodian government in August 2001 as its long-term plan for financial sector development.

Integrated Framework (IF)

Cambodia was selected among the LDCs to devise and implement a strategy aimed at "mainstreaming" trade into the national economic development plan.

- In 2001 the Ministry of Commerce, with the assistance of the World Bank and five other international agencies (IMF, UNDP, WTO, UNCTAD and ITC), carried out a pilot integration and competitiveness study to identify trade-related capacity building and technical assistance needs.

- In 2002, following the adoption of the Technical Assistance Matrix, several Trade Related Technical Assistance (TRTA) projects were launched by the five agencies and other donors, and are being implemented. The European Commission, in particular, is carrying out the Multilateral Trade Assistance Project (MULTRAP) that will provide technical assistance to the Cambodian government, coordinated by the Ministry of Commerce with regard to WTO accession, trade facilitation and diversification. Other EU countries such as France, Germany and the UK also support technical assistance projects in the trade area.

5.9 External trade

During the 1960s, Cambodia exported agricultural products, mainly rice, rubber and corn. During the years of conflict, foreign trade virtually collapsed. In the 1980s, trade was controlled by state-owned trading organisations. The state monopoly was abolished in 1987 and, from 1993 restrictions on international trade were largely removed.

The tariff regime was reformed in April 2001. High rates were reduced from 120% to 35%, and the number of bands was reduced from 12 to 4 (0%, 7%, 15% and 35%). For FDI approved projects (see chapter FDI below) import duty exemptions are being granted under the Law on Investment.

Cambodia's main exports are garments (75%), footwear (5%), wood products and rubber products. Imports mainly consist in textile materials for the garment industry, petroleum products, construction materials, vehicles and consumer goods.

In 2002, exports amounted to USD 1.77 billion whereas imports totalled USD 2.3 billion, resulting in a trade deficit of USD 544 million, up from a deficit of USD 527 million in 2001.

In 2003, exports amounted to USD 1.57 billion and imports decreased to USD 2.04 billion, resulting in a slightly lower deficit of USD 470 million.

5.10 Inflation and exchange rate

After experiencing very high rates of inflation from 1989 to 1993, the Cambodian government has succeeded in keeping prices under control since 1994, thanks to the stable link of the riel to the US dollar and to prudent financial and budgetary policies. From 1994 to 2000 the riel-denominated inflation was about 6% a year in Phnom Penh, and about 10% in the provinces due to high transportation costs. Over the last three years, the inflation rate has been kept below 5%.

	1999	2000	2001	2002
Inflation rate	4%	-0.8%	0.2%	3.3%
Current account balance (%GDP)	-8.9%	-12.3%	-13.4%	-10.7%

The riel/dollar conversion rate has been stable at about 4 000 riels to the USD since 1998, and foreign exchange reserves have increased from USD 390 million in 1998 to USD 780 million at the end of 2003, representing about 3.5 months of imports.

5.11 Fiscal reform and budget policy

Fiscal and budget management policies have been central elements of economic reform. The fiscal policy implemented in 1994 played a key role in restoring financial stability in Cambodia. However the government could not achieve its objective to increase budget revenues from 5.4% of GDP in

1993 to 15% by 2000, despite the successful introduction of the VAT, due to inefficiencies in the tax collection system.

The overall tax structure remains weak: revenue still relies heavily on taxing imported products, revenue from direct taxation accounting for only about 1% of GDP in 2000.

In 2002, the government had an overall fiscal deficit of 6.5%. Revenues accounted for 11.1% of GDP and total expenditures for 17.6%. Almost all the deficit was financed through concessionary lending and grants.

The structural adjustment loans and project loans from international financial institutions have been adding over recent years, resulting in a total debt of USD 558 million at the end of 2001. In addition, sizeable debts to the USA (USD 300 million) and to Russia (USD 1400 million) that were incurred by Cambodia in the 1970-1990 period are being contested by the government.

A Public Financial Management Reform programme is currently being developed which aims at improving tax collection and the management of public finances.

5.11.1 Financial sector reform

The financial sector is governed by the Law on Banking and Financial Institutions that was enacted in November 1999. The law provides the framework for the licensing, organisation, operation and supervision of a broad range of financial services companies, from commercial banks to micro-finance institutions, under the supervision of the National Bank of Cambodia (NBC).

In 2000, the Cambodian government initiated a major bank restructuring programme to re-license all the commercial banks based on higher capital requirements (above USD 13 million). The number of commercial banks was reduced from 31 to 13 in 2003. They included the state-owned Foreign Trade Bank, nine Locally Incorporated Banks, some of which have foreign banks from Thailand or Singapore as shareholders, and three Foreign Branch Banks that are branches of Thai and Malaysian banks. The only EU bank is the Standard Chartered Bank set up as a representative office.

The financial sector also includes a significant number of Micro Finance Institutions, with five licensed institutions and almost one hundred NGOs, 30 of them registered.

The Cambodian government enacted the Insurance Law in 2000. The law and implementing sub-decree of 2001 provide for compulsory insurance for commercial vehicles, construction and passenger transport. There are four insurance companies, including the state-owned Cambodian National Insurance Company.

There is no capital market yet in Cambodia. The government has created a working group and legislation is being drafted to establish a securities exchange commission that would eventually set up a stock exchange.

6. The business environment

Emerging from a long period of conflict, Cambodia is working towards reconstruction and economic development. The signing of the Paris Peace Accord in 1991 ended years of civil war and violence and allowed Cambodia to rebuild through the development of a market economy. Privatisation and liquidation of almost all state-owned enterprises took place in the 1990s, only a few remain today.

6.1 Private sector profile

Agriculture is the largest sector of the economy accounting for 77% of employment and 33.4% of GDP. The industrial sector has risen from 15.2% of GDP in 1997 to 26.3% in 2002, mainly due to the development of the garment industry that accounts for almost half of all industrial employment. The service sector, with tourism and trade as its main components, accounts for 34.2% of GDP and 15% of employment.

6.1.1 The informal sector

The informal sector is prevalent in Cambodia comprising over 80% of GDP and 95% of employment. Cambodia's enterprises are typically small, and often not integrated with global or even national markets. The majority are in service industries. In manufacturing, most are unregistered agro-industrial enterprises. The informal industrial sector is composed of over 27 000 small enterprises which are not registered with the Ministry of Commerce (MoC). Only half of these enterprises have operating licenses from the Ministry of Industry, Mines and Energy. Some larger enterprises, including a number that are foreign-owned, also operate without registration with the relevant authorities. The informal industrial sector, estimated to account for about half of total industrial output, supplies mainly the domestic market.

6.1.2 The formal sector

Registered private enterprises, estimated to number about 9 000, constitute the formal private sector. These enterprises acquire legal status as commercial enterprises through registration with the MoC and are required to pay profit tax based on the real regime calculation method, which relies on the submission of financial statements. Their legal status as commercial enterprises allows them to apply for import and export licenses and improves their access to the formal financial services sector. It also gives them access to investment incentives through the Law on Investment.

6.1.3 The foreign sector – Foreign Direct Investment (FDI)

Almost all companies with foreign direct investment (FDI), the "foreign sector", belong to the formal sector. The for-eign sector plays an important role in the Cambodian economy. It is the main source of exports.

FDI started in the early 1990s, with the construction of hotels needed by the United Nations Transitional Authority in Cambodia (UNTAC). With the enactment of the Investment Law in 1994 and, more importantly, due to its privileged access to the US and EU garment markets, Cambodia attracted a significant amount of FDI in the years 1996-2000. According to UNCTAD estimates, the annual average of actual FDI flows to Cambodia was USD 216.7 million during that period. In 2001 the actual FDI amount was estimated to be USD 148.1 million, whereas it was only USD 53.8 million in 2002. For 2003, the Cambodian Investment Board reported that it had approved 47 projects with a total investment of USD 250.1 million. From past experience, it may be expected that only about half these projects will be implemented.

FDI has been heavily concentrated in the garment industry, hotels and telecommunications.

The main sources of FDI have been Asian countries, primarily Malaysia, Taiwan, China, South Korea and Singapore. Japanese investors are notably absent from Cambodia.

Other investors include a few US companies and a number of European SMEs, the majority of which are French. Their presence is concentrated in the services sector (trading companies, hotels and restaurants, travel agencies and tour operators, forwarding services, engineering and architecture, consulting) and construction. Only a few larger EU firms have invested in Cambodia: BAT (UK) operates an integrated tobacco production facility, VINCI (France) owns and operates the Phnom Penh and Siem Reap airports, in partnership with a Malaysian company and Millicom International Cellulars (Sweden) operates one of the mobile telephone networks.

Two European banks, Standard Chartered and Credit Agricole Indosuez have recently decided to terminate the operations of their branches in Cambodia.

6.1.4 Business Organisations

Cambodia's main trade and industry organisations are the Cambodia Chamber of Commerce, the Cambodian Federation of Business Associations (CAMFEBA), the SME Association and the Garment Manufacturers Association of Cambodia (GMAC). Other sector specific business associations are being initiated and developed, such as rice millers' associations, the Hotel Owners Association and the Association of Banks in Cambodia.

Foreign business associations include the International Business Club of Cambodia and bi-lateral organisations such as the Franco-Khmer Chamber of Commerce, the German and the British Business Groups, the American

Business Association, the Malaysian Business Club and the Chinese Business Association.

6.1.5 Private Sector Forum

A government initiative called the Private Sector Forum, aimed at addressing investors' concerns, is designed as a bi-annual meeting of the Cambodian government and representatives of the private sector. It is comprised of seven sector-specific working groups:

- energy and infrastructure,
- banking and finance,
- manufacturing and distribution,
- agro-industry and food processing,
- tourism,
- export processing and law,
- tax and good governance.

6.2 Legal and regulatory framework

6.2.1 Laws on the enterprise and financial sectors

In recent years the government has made progress in creating the legal framework for the development of the private sector. The main laws that have been enacted are:

- The Law on Banking and Financial Institutions in 1999
- The Insurance Law in 2000
- The new Land Law in 2001
- The Law on Mineral Resources Management in 2001
- The Law on the Adoption and Implementation of United Nations Convention on the Recognition and Enforcement of Foreign Arbitral Awards and the Law on the Adoption of the Convention on the Settlement of Investment Disputes between States and Nationals of other States in 2001
- The Trademarks Law in 2002.
- The Law on Enterprise Accounting and Auditing in 2002

Moreover, the government has drafted the Law on Commercial Enterprises and submitted it to the National Assembly in June 2002. The government has also approved a law on commercial arbitration, which will be submitted to the National Assembly. The government is drafting commercial contract legislation, a law on insolvency and a law on negotiable instruments and payment transactions. It is also preparing a law on secured transactions, which will play an essential role in improving companies' access to bank financing by strengthening the collateral system.

In addition, the government has drafted an important law to establish a Commercial Court, which is expected to be examined by the National Assembly in 2005.

Several laws that have a bearing on private sector development are also pending the resumption of legislative work:

- The Anti-corruption Law
- The Law on Customs
- The Tourism Law
- The Law on Factory Management
- The Law on Industrial Zones

6.2.2 WTO

In September 2003, the WTO Ministerial Conference in Cancun approved Cambodia's accession to the WTO. The Protocol of Accession to the WTO was approved by the National Assembly and the Senate in September 2004. Cambodia became a full member of WTO in October 2004.

The full text of Cambodia's commitments is provided in Annex 1.

The main commitments are as follows:

- **Textiles regime:** Textiles and clothing import quotas that other members apply to import from Cambodia will have growth rates applied as provided for in the Agreement on Textiles and Clothing, from the date of accession. These growth rates will end when the Agreement on Textiles and Clothing terminates (end 2004).

- **Agricultural products:** Cambodia agreed to bind its agricultural export subsidies at zero, and to refrain from applying any export subsidy for agricultural products.

- **Export subsidies:** Cambodia will comply with the Subsidies Agreement from accession. It will either eliminate the existing system of remission of import fees and waiver of duty for certain goods used by certain investors, or establish a duty drawback system consistent with WTO provisions, through amendment of the Law on Investment, as necessary, by the end of 2013.

- **Rules of origin:** Cambodia will comply with the provisions of the WTO rules of origin Agreement by 1 January 2005.

- **Trade-related aspects of intellectual property (TRIPS):** Cambodia will apply the TRIPS Agreement by 1 January 2007.

- **Technical Barriers to Trade (TBT):** Cambodia will rely on the provisions of the TBT Agreement from 1 January 2007.

- **Sanitary and phytosanitary measures (SPS):** Cambodia will gradually implement the SPS Agreement will full implementation by 1 January 2008.

- **Customs valuation:** Cambodia will implement the customs valuation Agreement from 1 January 2009.

Cambodia has also made a number of commitments relating to its institutions, in particular to step up reforms in its legislative and judicial systems. An ambitious schedule has been set out to enact a total of 47 new laws and regulations by 2006 in order to fulfil WTO membership requirements (see Annex 2: schedule of WTO-related laws). As listed above, some of them have already been approved by the government and are pending the resumption of work by the new legislature to be enacted by parliament.

6.2.3 ASEAN

Cambodia's membership in the Association of Southeast Asian Nations (ASEAN) will also have a deep impact on its legal and regulatory framework. As ASEAN moves towards economic integration, with the objective of achieving the goal of an ASEAN Economic Community by 2020, business activities in the region will increasingly be guided by a set of common rules and practices. This is particularly the case in the area of standards and conformance, where ASEAN member countries are progressing towards harmonising national standards with international standards and implementing mutual recognition arrangements on conformity assessment.

6.2.4 The Law on Investment

The investment regime was defined in 1994 by the Law on Investment (LOI). This law was amended in February 2003.

The main elements of the LOI are the following:

- The Council for the Development of Cambodia (CDC) is the government agency that oversees Cambodia's investment policy and approves investment projects. It consists of two executive boards, the Cambodian Rehabilitation and Development Board (CRDB) and the Cambodian Investment Board (CIB). The CDRB is responsible for public investment and the coordination of international assistance, the CIB is responsible for dealing with private investment. The CDC's Executive Committee is co-chaired by the Prime Minister and the President of the National Assembly and comprises three Vice-Chairmen (Minister of Economy and Finance, Minister of Commerce, Secretary of State of Economy and Finance), the Secretary General of the CDC, the Secretary General of the CDRB and the Secretary General of the CIB. The Cambodian Investment Board (CIB) is the operational arm of the CDC. It is responsible for the evaluation and facilitation ("one-stop service") of investment projects.

- The LOI guarantees investors neither to nationalise foreign-owned assets, nor to establish price controls on goods produced or services rendered by investors.

- The LOI also guarantees that investors can freely remit foreign currencies abroad for the purposes of paying imported goods and services, paying loan principal and interest to foreign banks, paying royalties and management fees, remitting profit and repatriating capital on dissolution of investment projects.

- The LOI specifies that investors can set up 100% foreign-owned investment projects and employ qualified managerial personnel, technical staff and skilled workers.

- Only Qualified Investment Projects (QIPs) are entitled to the benefits of the new LOI. In order to qualify as a QIP, an investment project must be granted a Final Registration Certificate (FRC). To obtain an FRC, the intending investors must submit an Investment Proposal to the CDC in the required form. Within three business days of receipt of the Investment proposal, the CDC will issue to the applicant a Conditional Registration Certificate (CRC) or a Letter of Non-Compliance. If the CDC fails to issue a CRC or a Letter of Non-Compliance within these three days, the CRC will be taken to have been approved.

- The CRC will state the approvals, authorisations, licences and permits required for the QIP to operate, as well as the government entities responsible for issuing such approvals. The CRC will also confirm the incentives granted to the QIP. The Final Registration Certificate (FRC) must be issued within 28 business days of the date of issue of the CRC. The CDC is required to provide a "one-stop service" by obtaining such approvals for the investor.

The main incentives available to QIPs are the following:

- An automatic **tax holiday of three years,** with up to three additional years depending on the activity or sector, the tax holiday to commence with the first year in which profit is made but not later than the fourth year of operation.

- Domestically-oriented **QIPs are exempted from import duties** on production equipment and production input construction materials.

- **Export-oriented QIPs are exempted from import duties** on production equipment, construction materials, intermediate goods and production input accessories.

- **Supporting industry QIPs are exempted from import duties** on production equipment, construction materials, raw materials, intermediate goods and production input accessories.

6.3 The Tax system

The Cambodian tax system is governed by the Taxation Law of 1997 which establishes the regime for profit, salary, value-added and excise taxes. The tax system divides taxpayers into two regimes, the real regime and the estimated regime based on the form of the enterprise, its activity and the level of its sales turnover. All limited liability companies fall under the real regime, with profit taxes calculated on the basis of audited financial statements.

The Taxation Law was amended in 1999 to include the Value Added Tax (VAT), and it was amended again in February 2003.

The main features of the new law are as follows:

6.3.1 Corporate profit tax (real regime)

Tax rate

The tax on profit is 20% for all taxpayers, except certain natural resources development projects, but including all Qualified Investment Projects (QIPs), e.g. FDI projects approved by the CDC. Pre-existing QIPs that have been granted a 9% tax rate will keep the benefit of the reduced rate, only for five years. QIPs that have been granted a tax exemption will benefit from the 0% rate for a maximum period of 9 years (trigger period + 3 years + priority period where the trigger period is the earlier of the first year of profit or three years after the QIP earns its first revenue).

Minimum tax

A minimum tax is imposed on all taxpayers registered under the real regime at the rate of 1% of annual turnover. QIPs are exempt from this minimum tax.

Prepayment of tax on profit

Taxpayers liable for profit tax under the real regime as well as QIPs subject to 9% profit tax have to make monthly tax prepayments at the rate of 1% of turnover of the previous month, inclusive of all taxes except VAT. QIPs with tax exemptions are exempted from this prepayment.

Tax on dividends

QIPs that enjoy a tax rate of 9% or that are exempted from profit tax will have to pay an additional tax of 20% upon distribution of dividends, effectively pushing the tax on profit to 20%.

Special depreciation

Purchase of capital equipment by QIPs are eligible for a special depreciation rate of 40% during the year of purchase if the QIPs do not elect the profit tax exemption.

6.3.2 Salary tax

Salaries paid by employers to employees are taxed at rates from 5 to 20% (see table). There is a distinction between residents and non-residents: residents (persons who either (a) are domiciled in Cambodia, (b) have a principal place of abode in Cambodia, (c) are physically present in Cambodia for at least 182 days in the year) are taxable on their worldwide income, whereas non-residents are subject to tax only on Cambodian source salary, at a flat rate of 20%.

Employers are required to pay a fringe benefit tax on benefits provided to employees, at a rate of 20% of the market value of the benefits, inclusive of all taxes.

6.3.3 Withholding tax

The 1997 Taxation Law introduced the following withholding taxes (some rates were modified by the amended 2003 Law):

Local payments

- 15% on payments made to individuals for services provided (eg. management, consulting)

- 15% on payments of royalties for intangibles, oil, gas, minerals and interest (except interest paid to domestic banks)

- 10% on payments for rental of movable and immovable property

- 6% on interest paid by a domestic bank or savings institution to a resident taxpayer having a fixed-term deposit account

- 4% on interest paid by a local bank to a resident taxpayer with a non-fixed-term savings account

Foreign payments

A withholding tax rate of 14% must be withheld on the following payments to non-residents, whether overseas or within Cambodia:

- Interest

- Royalties, rent and other income related to the use of property

- Payment of management and technical services

- Dividends

6.3.4 Indirect taxes

Import and export duties

All goods imported to Cambodia are subject to duties as set by the Customs Department under the Customs Tariff Schedule. Duties range between 0% and 35%.

At present there are no export duties applied in Cambodia, other than those levied on restricted export products such as timber, rubber and seafood.

Excise duties

Excise duty is called "tax on specific goods and services". It applies to a wide range of imported or domestically produced goods and services including vehicles, petroleum products, alcoholic beverages and tobacco.

Value-added tax

A value-added tax (VAT) was introduced on January 1, 1999. It is chargeable on a wide range of goods and services supplied in Cambodia and on the import of goods. The VAT rate is 10%.

Exported goods and services are not subject to VAT.

6.4 The Labour Law & salaries

6.4.1 Content of law

The Labour Law was enacted in 1997. It guarantees the rights for workers to organise the right to strike through labour unions and associations, in accordance with set rules. It provides for collective bargaining agreements and dispute resolution procedures, and sets requirements for overtime, night work and holiday pay. It also includes provisions for work place safety and requirements on work place injuries. Labour inspectors, controllers and medical inspectors are allowed to freely enter an enterprise without prior notification.

Foreign companies have virtually unrestricted access to Cambodia's labour force. There are no restrictions on employing Cambodian workers with proper documentation. The employment of foreigners is allowed with few restrictions, particularly for QIPs. There are no limitations on appointing foreigners to higher level positions, but a ceiling of 10% foreigners of total work force is imposed with exceptions being made upon a showing of need to the Ministry of Labour.

The Labour Law makes provisions for the settlement of individual and collective labour disputes. In the event of a collective dispute, the Labour Inspector is notified and the Ministry of Labour is required to appoint a mediator within 24 hours. Mediation can last up to 15 days. If mediation fails, the dispute is resolved through the provisions of the collective bargaining agreement. In case of failure, the dispute must be resolved within 15 days by an Arbitration Panel appointed by the Ministry of Labour.

6.4.2 Average of salaries

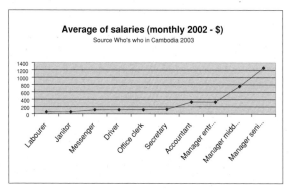

Average of salaries (monthly 2002 - $)
Source Who's who in Cambodia 2003

Source: Who's Who in Cambodia 2003.

6.5 Constraints for the private sector

The growth of the private sector in Cambodia over the past ten years has been remarkable. Privately-owned industry, in particular, which had been practically non-existent until 1993, has been growing at a yearly rate of about 10% since 1995.

The garment sector in particular has experienced a spectacular growth, from a turnover of about USD 20 million in

1995 to over USD 1 billion in 2002. Yet this growth has been heavily concentrated in a few sectors and areas, and has lacked integration and linkage to the broader economy. The substantial FDI flows seen in the garment, tourism and telecommunications sectors responded to specific opportunities, such as the privileged access to the EU and US markets for garments.

In other sectors (spinning, weaving, dyeing and finishing, chemicals, mechanical industries, food-processing, electrical and electronic industries, etc.) there has been practically no investment, either domestic or foreign. However, the Cambodian government expects to attract FDI in the above-mentioned sectors, by setting up some industrial zones in Sihanoukville and along the Thai-Cambodian border. The works for the physical construction of these industrial sites will start in 2005.

6.5.1 Legal and judicial environment

Despite the government's efforts, the legal and regulatory framework for the private sector remains weak. After laws are passed, there are long delays in enacting the required sub-decrees. Without judicial reform to assure enforcement of laws and regulations the legal reforms remain largely ineffective. The successful implementation of the legal and regulatory framework will require a strong commitment and decisive action by the government.

6.5.2 Physical infrastructure

At present, Cambodia's infrastructure is not able to respond to the needs of economic development, both in terms of coverage and in terms of quality and efficiency.

Roads are the only mode of transport with a nationwide network. The network is about 34 000 km, out of which 10 400 km are usable by motor vehicles, and only 2 000 km consist in asphalted roads in good condition

With only 591 km of tracks and limited rolling stock, the rail service is a marginal player in the transportation of people and goods in Cambodia.

Cambodia's only deep seaport is at Sihanoukville. Its present capacity is limited, but it is undertaking a large-scale expansion. Its costs are among the highest in Asia.

Cambodia has a low electrification rate and a high cost of electricity (USD 15 cents per kW hr, about 2.5 times the international average).

The telecommunications sector has undergone significant change over the last decade. There were about 100 000 telephone lines in 2000, four companies offer mobile phone services and internet access is available in most cities. Yet, the combined fixed and mobile phone penetration rate is only 1.54 per 100 habitants, a low level by international and regional standards.

6.5.3 High costs

The cost of doing business in Cambodia is high. The high cost of electricity affects production costs; while expensive fuel and inadequate roads increase the cost of transportation, as do both official and unofficial highway charges. A recent World Bank study on the supply chain in the garment industry has shown that export procedures account for about USD 400 in administration costs for each container of clothes shipped abroad.

The high cost of port facilities and import administration combined with import duties and VAT, increase the costs of imported inputs. The high cost of inputs severely affects the competitiveness of Cambodian products in domestic and foreign markets.

Labour costs are not the lowest in the Asian region. In the garment industry, the average monthly wage is USD 61, higher than in India or Indonesia.

SALARY IN THE CAMBODIAN GARMENT SECTOR IN COMPARISON WITH OTHER COUNTRIES IN THE REGION

Country	Wage (per month)	Year
Bangladesh	40	1996
Indonesia	40	1999
India	57	1999
Vietnam	60	2000
Cambodia	**61**	**2000**
Sri Lanka	63	1998
Thailand	106	1999
Philippines	182	1999
China	191	1997
Malaysia	296	1995

Source: US Department of Labor and Bureau of International Labor Affairs.

6.5.4 Market access

Local manufacturers face unfair competition in the domestic market from imported goods, particularly from smuggled goods which enter the country without import duty and VAT taxes. Smuggling has been identified as the most important problem faced by Cambodian manufacturers in maintaining competitiveness.

Trade facilitation practices are cumbersome and superfluous; they involve the payment of formal and informal costs payments and result in long delays. The current situation, however, is likely to improve with the setting up of a single window and the customs automation, which is expected to be implemented by the end of 2005.

The access to foreign markets is difficult and expensive due to the poor infrastructure and to the high costs of export processing. On the other hand, WTO membership, ASEAN integration and RTAs will offer great opportunity in terms of market access to Cambodian products. At the same time, the infrastructure is being improved, including the extension of the Sihanoukville Port.

6.5.5 Access to financing

Cambodian firms have limited access to bank financing.

High liquidity requirements and the absence of an appropriate legal framework for secured transactions make it difficult for banks to fully play their role in lending to the economy. Because of limited competition and the high risk of lending, banks only lend to well-known and trusted firms. Hence only larger enterprises make use of banking facilities, the large majority of SMEs relying on their own resources or on informal external sources for their funding.

Other forms of financing, such as leasing are not yet available in Cambodia.

With the support of international institutions, the RGC is working to improve the regulatory framework, which is a necessary prerequisite for an efficient financing sector.

It is expected that the government's financial sector development plan, to be implemented over the 2001-2010 period, will gradually result in a sound, market-based financial system that will meet the needs of Cambodian companies.

6.5.6 Land tenure

Land tenure is a serious problem for the private sector due to the limited level of land titling in the country. While the Land Law provides the legal framework for land tenure, land titling needs further implementation as do mechanisms for enforcing the law, reducing land conflicts and facilitating land management.

6.5.7 Standards and quality

There is little awareness in Cambodia of quality and standards issues, except in the export-oriented industries like the garment industry and in a few companies who deal with export markets.

One of the reasons is the absence of relevant legislation. This is notably the case in the area of food products, where some potential export destinations, such as the EU, require that a complete set of laws and regulations be complied with.

The Cambodian government has started to address this problem and laws are being drafted on metrology, industrial standards and Sanitary & Phyto-Sanitary Measures. Another reason is the weakness of the institutional set-up as the concerned institutions, the Ministry of Industry, Mines and Energy, the Ministry of Agriculture, Forestry and Fisheries and the Ministry of Commerce through its specialised agency CAMCONTROL lack resources and capacity to effectively perform their functions. This is also being addressed, notably with technical assistance programmes provided by international donors. The European Commission, in particular, is active in this area through a regional programme, "the EU-ASEAN Standards and Quality Co-operation Programme".

7. Positive factors

7.1 Physical infrastructure

The government, with the assistance of many donors and the notable participation of the private sector, has been working to improve the country's physical infrastructure.

7.1.1 Roads

The network of major highways linking Phnom Penh with the main cities of Battambang, Siem Reap, Sihanoukville, and with Thailand, Vietnam and Laos is being built or rehabilitated with the financial assistance of the ADB, the World Bank and bilateral aid from Japan, Thailand and China. A number of road projects are planned and financed in the framework of the Greater Mekong Sub-region (GMS) programme. This key network, many sections of which are already completed, will be fully operational within three years. One of the major benefits of the new network will be to allow travel from Bangkok to Phnom-Penh and Ho Chi Minh Ville in a few hours.

7.1.2 Electricity

The improvement of electricity supply is carried out under the Power Sector Strategy. The long-term plan is to build a high-voltage grid in the area west of Phnom Penh and Tonle Sap, connecting to Vietnam in the south and Thailand in the north-west which will allow the importation of cheaper power from Vietnam and Thailand. In the short term, the Cambodian government relies on the private sector to build and operate power plants. Several Power Purchase Agreements (PPA) have been concluded in recent years between Electricité du Cambodge and private operators who produce electricity in Phnom Penh and in several provincial centres.

In the rural areas, the World Bank and the ADB are developing rural electrification projects.

7.1.3 Airports

Cambodia's two international airports, Phnom Penh and Siem Reap, have been contracted out for development and management to a French-Malaysian joint-venture.

The Phnom Penh airport has been renovated and expanded, the Siem Reap airport will have a new terminal by 2005. The renovation and management of the Sihanoukville airport has been contracted to a Malaysian company, and it was reopened in 2004.

7.1.4 Ports

Cambodia's only seaport at Sihanoukville is undertaking a large-scale expansion including the construction of a 400-meter quay for general cargo, a container terminal and a bulk cargo terminal. The Prime Minister has recently declared that Cambodia has adopted the "open-sea policy", which should result in the construction of other minor ports. A private port is being completed in Kho Kong and is expected to be used mainly for cattle and agro-export.

7.1.5 Telecommunications

Cambodia's modest expansion of fixed lines networks has been compensated by a rapid growth of mobile phone services, largely contracted out to foreign investors, which now cover most of the country. Likewise, internet services are widely available in Phnom Penh and the main provincial cities.

7.2 Work force and labour conditions

The Cambodian work force is reputed to be able and willing. It is motivated to learn and is capable of creativity and flexibility.

Employment is governed by the 1997 Labour Law, drafted with the assistance of the International Labour Organisation-(ILO), which meets international social standards. The compliance with these standards has been a key element in allowing the Cambodian garment industry to gain privileged access to the USA.

7.3 Access to the EU

Cambodia was granted Most Favoured Nation (MFN) status by the EU in 1993, which gave it equally privileged access to EU markets as GATT members. Since then, Cambodia has never been subject to quota restrictions by the EU.

EBA

In its trade with the EU, Cambodia benefits from the Generalised Scheme of Preferences (GSP) that provides tariff reductions without quantitative limitations. As a "Least Developed Country - LDC" Cambodia is entitled to benefit from the most favourable treatment under the GSP, the so-called "Everything But Arms – EBA" provisions (European Council Regulation No. 2501/2001).

Under the EBA Cambodia is entitled to duty-free and quota-free access to the EU for all its exports, except arms and ammunitions. Only the imports into the EU of fresh bananas, rice and sugar are not fully liberalised immediately. The duties on these products will be gradually reduced: duty free access will be granted for bananas in January 2006, for sugar in July 2009 and for rice in September

2009. In the meantime, there will be duty free tariff quotas for rice and sugar. These quotas will increase annually. The rules for opening and administration of the annual tariff quotas for rice and sugar are detailed in Commission regulations No 1401/2002 and No 1381/2002 respectively.

Although EBA is part of the EU's GSP scheme, it is not subject to its periodic renewal. Therefore the date of expiry of the current GSP cycle (2004) does not apply to the EBA provisions.

Rules of Origin

In order to benefit from the EBA, Cambodian exports to the EU must prove their Cambodian originating status in accordance with the rules of origin, as laid down in Commission Regulation (EEC) No 2454/93, and amended by Regulations Nos. 12/97, 1602/2000 and 881/2003.

While products that are fully produced in Cambodia are naturally considered as originating there, products manufactured with inputs from other countries are considered so only if they have undergone sufficient working or processing in Cambodia.

In order to foster regional integration, the EC has allowed the rules of origin to include the possibility of regional accumulation of origin between the members of regional groups. Cambodia belonging to the ASEAN, is therefore allowed to treat materials and inputs originating in other ASEAN countries (except Burma/Myanmar) as if they were originating in Cambodia (on condition that the working or processing and value added are sufficient).

The GSP rules of origin for textiles require that, for the products to be considered as originating, they must be obtained after two stages of processing. A derogation currently allows Cambodian producers to export textile garments (with GSP Cambodian originating status) obtained after only one processing operations from materials originating not only in ASEAN (except Burma/Myanmar) countries but also in SAARC or ACP countries.

7.4 Access to the USA

The access to the US market has evolved over the last 6-7 years. Before 1996, the market was de facto closed to Cambodian garments due to high tariff rates. In October 1996, the USA granted Cambodia the MFN status with a privileged tariff rate. Faced with a steep surge of imports, the USA changed their position in 1997 and granted Cambodia the GSP status, thereby excluding it from the MFN privileges. Further, the USA established a quota system, which is still valid today. In 1999, the USA and Cambodia reached an agreement whereby quotas would be increased at an annual minimum rate of 6%, with the possibility of additional increments of up to 24% depending upon Cambodia's performance with regard to labour standards. In fact, quotas were increased by 9% in 2000, by 14% in 2001 and by 18% for 2003.

Cambodia's accession to the WTO should allow an equal treatment with other LDCs.

7.5 Regional integration

ASEAN

Cambodia is a member of ASEAN, the Association of South-East Asian Nations. The 10 member countries have a population of about 550 million. ASEAN is engaged in an economic integration process, including the Asian Free Trade Area (AFTA) under which tariff rates are being reduced to 0-5%. This reduction will apply to Cambodia by 2010.

At their summit in October 2003 in Bali, the ASEAN leaders have agreed on the Bali Concord II, a declaration of intent to establish an ASEAN Community based on the three pillars of political and security cooperation, economic cooperation and socio-cultural cooperation.

In the area of economic cooperation, the establishment of the Asian Economic Community is set as the end-goal of **economic integration by the year 2020.** Of particular relevance to Cambodia are the objectives to address the development divide and accelerate the economic integration of Asian's less-developed countries, and to work towards integrating industries across the region to promote regional sourcing.

Greater Mekong Sub-region

At the sub-regional level, Cambodia belongs to the Greater Mekong Sub-region (GMS), a programme involving Laos, Burma/Myanmar, Thailand, Vietnam and the Yunnan Province of China. This programme, launched in 1992 with the support of the Asian Development Bank, mainly aims at developing infrastructure projects that will greatly enhance the overall economic growth of the region.

7.6 WTO accession

As described above (section 6.2.2), Cambodia is a new member of the WTO.

Cambodia's primary objective in acceding to the WTO is to integrate its economy in the international market structure, by securing a rules-based market access. WTO membership was vital for enabling the garment industry to remain in the country after the removal of export quotas at the end of 2004, with the end of the Multi-Fibre Agreement (MFA).

By joining the WTO, Cambodia will also be able to benefit from rights accorded to all members such as non-discrimination by other members (Most Favoured Nation treatment) and access to the dispute settlement procedure. Cambodia will benefit from the Goods Dispute Settlement Mechanisms that aim to protect small and vulnerable economies from being violated by the large ones.

Further to these short term potential benefits in the trade area, an important positive consequence of WTO accession for Cambodia should be the far-reaching legal reforms that the government has committed to implement.

Viewed from a business perspective, WTO accession will represent a major challenge for the Cambodian private sector that will need to improve its competitiveness in order to be able to face acute international competition, particularly from countries like China and India.

7.7 Geo-strategic position

Cambodia is located between Thailand and Vietnam, two dynamic countries with substantial populations and markets. These two countries stand at different stages of development and can offer a wide range of co-operation opportunities to Cambodian enterprises, within the context of ASEAN's integration policies.

In a wider perspective, Cambodia is located in the centre of the Greater Mekong River Basin Region that is set to develop its full potential once major communication infrastructure projects are completed.

PART II

Sector Profiles:

**Potential for EU-Cambodia
business co-operation**

8. Tourism

8.1 General description

Cambodia lies at the heart of the ancient Khmer Empire that dominated Southeast Asia from the 9th to the 15th centuries. A symbol of Cambodia's civilisation of that time, the Angkor Wat Archaeological Park, is recognised today as one of the most remarkable historical sites of the world and it attracts increasing numbers of tourists from all over the globe. In addition to Angkor and other ancient sites, potentials for developing tourism activities exists in the following areas:

• forests and natural parks;
• ecological resources, such as wild animals, river dolphins and bird sanctuaries;
• beaches and islands.

Tourism has grown remarkably since 1993, with particular strong growth since 1999 due to improved security and infrastructure. The number of tourist arrivals increased from 368 000 to 786 000 between 1999 and 2002. In 2003, the Iraq war and the SARS epidemic severely disrupted the industry, resulting in a decrease of arrivals (701 014, according to Ministry of Tourism's figures). For 2004, the figures of the first semester (448 239 arrivals) point to a strong rebound of growth, which is expected to continue over the next years.

The Siem Reap area alone, where the Angkor Wat Archaeological Complex is located, received about 450 000 foreign visitors in 2002, which accounts for about 57% of all foreign tourists.

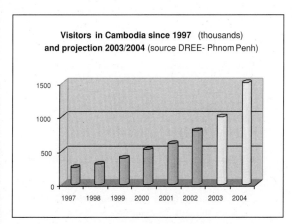

Source: DREE- Phnom Penh & Ministry of Tourism.

* The SARS crisis has reduced tourist arrivals in 2003, but the figures of the first quarter of 2004 indicate a recovery of the sector with 450 000 visitors.

Besides restored security and improved infrastructure, several factors have helped in facilitating the arrival of tourists, mainly the open skies policy and the possibility to obtain visas on arrival.

Cambodia has developed a policy of "open skies" and the two main airports have increased the international flights.

The policy seems to have worked well, despite criticism that it favours Siem Reap at the expense of other places in Cambodia, including Phnom Penh. Also, the policy seems to have mostly benefited foreign operators/owners of hotels and airlines rather than the local population.

Hospitality facilities have expanded to meet the demand. The number of hotels has increased from 125 in 1993 to 292 (13 169 rooms) in 2003. Since 1994, total investment in hotels has amounted to around USD 660 million. Several European operators have been active in this development, like the European ACCOR group, Le Meridien and other smaller companies including a number of individual entrepreneurs.

Location	Hotels	Rooms	Guest houses	Guest house rooms
Phnom Penh	126	5 795	113	1 614
Sihanoukville	42	1 234	54	485
Siem reap (Angkhor)	62	2 722	100	1 018
Others	62	1 675	203	2 417
Total	**268**	**11 426**	**470**	**5 534**

Source: Ministry of Tourism of Cambodia (French DREE publication).

These capacities are occupied at a level of 38 - 40% (it is increasing from 30% in 1997 to 40% in 2001). This could be improved along the year, because there is a low season from May to October which hides a very good filling rate in high season from November to March.

Origin of visitors

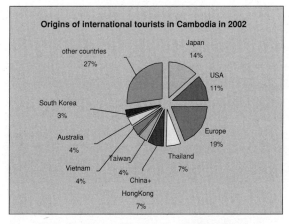

Source: Cambodian Ministry of Tourism - French DREE publication.

Considering the numbers of tourists visiting Thailand (about 10 million in 2002) and Vietnam (about 4,5 million), there is every reason to believe that Cambodia has the potential to become a major destination in its own right, especially given its unique asset, the Angkor Wat Archaeological Park.

Beside Cambodia's archaeological resources, good potential exists to develop eco-tourism, by helping to preserve natural resources, including the national parks, wild life sanctuaries and both the Tonle Sap biodiversity rich wetland eco-system and the coastal eco-systems, which are still relatively well sheltered. The existence of a large number of endangered wild animal species, including fresh water dolphins, is an indicator that the natural eco-system of Cambodia remains in pristine condition.

8.2 Legal and regulatory framework

A Tourism Law has been prepared by the government. When enacted, it is expected that it will include the following main provisions:

- The main purpose of the law would be to set the minimum safety standards for the customers. These mandatory standards would be enforced through a licensing system that will relate to (a) the manager of the service provider, (b) the premises, (c) the equipment, (d) the personnel, (e) insurance matters.

- The licensing system will be streamlined so that the implementing sub-decrees for the respective types of tourism activities will all be structured according to the same model.

- The scope of the law will include travel, entertainment and recreation.

- The types of tourism activities on which the licensing requirement applies will be based on internationally recognised classification systems. They will relate to (a) accommodation services, (b) food and beverage catering, (c) passenger transport and related services, (d) intermediaries and information services, (e) leisure activities.

- The law will include a system of hotel classification. A sub-decree on this issue was recently adopted.

- It will also spell out the rights and duties of tourism operators in a "Code of Ethics for Tourism".

8.3 Main actors

8.3.1 Transportation

The two main means of transportation for foreign tourists visiting Cambodia are by road and by air.

Road transportation
Road transportation is mainly used by visitors from neighbouring countries, Thailand and Vietnam, and by travellers inside Cambodia. A number of private bus companies operate services between Phnom Penh and the main provincial cities, and to Bangkok and Ho Chi Minh City.

Airlines and airports
Other visitors arrive by plane. The two main airports open to international air traffic are the Phnom Penh International Airport and, since 1998, the Siem Reap airport following the government's "open-skies" policy decision. Whilst this policy contributed to the development of tourism in Siem Reap, it stimulated competition between local and regional airlines at the expense of the Cambodian carriers. Some Cambodian private airlines operate in Cambodia: President Airlines, Royal Phnom Penh Airways and First Cambodia fly from Phnom Penh to Siem Reap, Bangkok and other local and regional destinations. A few regional carriers have regular flights to Phnom Penh and Siem Reap.

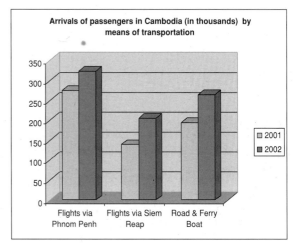

Source: Cambodian Ministry of Tourism.

Most foreign visitors, therefore, fly into Cambodia on foreign airlines from the main regional hubs in Thailand, Singapore, Malaysia, Vietnam, Japan and China.

The Phnom Penh and Siem Reap airports are managed by CAMS, a French-Malaysian joint-venture under contract with SCA (Société Concessionaire de l'Aéroport), another French-Malaysian company that entered into a Build-Operate-Transfer (BOT) contract with the Cambodian government in 1995 to upgrade and operate the Phnom Penh airport for a period of 25 years. The contract was subsequently extended to include the Siem Reap airport. The Phnom Penh airport has been expanded and upgraded to international standards; the Siem Reap airport will be upgraded with a new terminal by 2005.

The other airports in Cambodia are in Sihanoukville, which has been renovated and is being managed by a Malaysian company, and the smaller airports of Battambang, Mondulkiri, Rattanakiri and Stung Treng. Plans are underway to upgrade the latter two airports.

Boat transportation

Water transportation is an area of great potential in Cambodia with its unique waterways, the Mekong river and the Tonle Sap lake. For the time being, only a few companies offer boat services from Phnom Penh to Siem Reap, or to other destinations including Ho Chi Minh City. This will undoubtedly develop with better infrastructure, in particular with the renovation and expansion of the Phnom Penh port and the construction of a port on the Tonle Sap lake near Siem Reap.

8.3.2 Hotels

As seen above, the supply of hotel accommodation has increased substantially in Phnom Penh and Siem Reap to meet the growing demand of visitors. In other locations, the availability of hotels is still limited.

The owners and operators of hotels are quite diverse. Most are owned and managed by Cambodian and/or regional investors and operators. Only a few, particularly in the higher quality bracket, are run by international hotel management companies such as ACCOR, InterContinental and Raffles International. A few small/mid-size hotels, particularly in Siem Reap, have been set up by individual entrepreneurs, some of them Europeans, with apparent success. Even though the present capacity of hotel rooms in Phnom Penh and Siem Reap seems to be sufficient, or even to exceed the foreseeable short-term demand, the diversity and quality of accommodation appears to be insufficient. This is particularly the case in Siem Reap where only a few resort-type hotels are now operating.

8.3.3 Travel agents, tour operators

There are about 250 travel agencies in Cambodia, the large majority being owned and/or operated by Cambodians and offering basic ticketing services. Only a small number of travel service companies offer more sophisticated services such as the organisation of tailor-made travels, the design and organisation of packaged tours and inbound services. Among these, there are a few foreign-owned and operated firms, some of them being local offices of international travel organisations.

8.3.4 Business associations

Several associations have been established over recent years to represent the interests of tourism operators. The most active are the Phnom Penh Hotels Association, the Siem Reap Angkor Hotels and Guesthouses Association, the Cambodian Association of Travel Agents.

8.4 Strengths and weaknesses in Tourism sector

The strengths of the Cambodian tourism sector are as follows:

- The Angkor Wat Archaeological Park is reputed as one of the most remarkable historical sites of the world. It is under the close attention of the international community who has demonstrated its willingness to assist in its safeguard and enhancement.

- Cambodia has other cultural sites, interesting cities and a variety of attractive natural sites to offer, including mountains, lakes and rivers, forests and seaside locations.

- The Khmer cultural heritage is rich, as reflected in performing arts and handicrafts.

- Cambodia has been largely untouched by industrial activities and can boast an image of pollution-free, "green" country.

Its current weaknesses are:

- Most of the tourism growth takes place in Siem Reap/Angkor, and benefits foreign operators (airlines, hotel operators, suppliers of imported inputs) more then Cambodians. The growth of visitors in Siem Reap/Angkor may also result in the historical sites, and the Siem Reap city itself being overcrowded and spoilt.

- The average stay of foreign visitors is short, less than three days. It is often included as part of package tours featuring Thailand or Vietnam as the main destination. One of the main reasons is the lack of attractive, well-designed facilities in other locations such as the southern coast or the mountains. Another reason is the lack of promotion of alternative/additional destinations such as the city of Phnom Penh.

- Cambodia lacks infrastructure, particularly roads, electricity and accommodation facilities, especially in the more remote areas where ecotourism could be developed.

- Cambodia lacks skilled human resources, much education and training will be necessary to improve service delivery.

- The tourism regulatory framework is weak, without a tourism law and an appropriate authority to assure that quality facilities and services are provided.

- Cambodia is viewed by operators as one of the more expensive destinations in Asia: due to limited competition, especially on the Bangkok-Cambodia routes, plane fares are relatively high, and visa charges, entrance tickets to the Angkor Archaeological Park and other charges add up to result in rather costly stays.

8.5 Opportunities for EU companies

European tourism-related companies are reputed for their experience and the quality of their services. They are well placed to take part in the development of tourism in Cambodia in the following areas:

- Equipment and services: EU companies can supply a wide range of goods and services to the developers of hotels and other facilities. In fact a number of European architects, designers and contractors based in Cambodia are active in this area. Likewise trading companies based in Phnom Penh, some of which are EU-owned and managed can provide equipment, building materials and components.

- Distributing Cambodian products: EU tour operators and travel agents can distribute travel products designed and delivered by Cambodian firms, or by European-Cambodian companies based in Cambodia. A few firms based in Phnom Penh are working in this field, offering package tours of up to two weeks exclusively in

Cambodia. Considering the interest of EU travellers in cultural discoveries, this area is felt to have a good potential.

• Technical assistance and management services: EU companies can provide consulting services to Cambodian firms and investors who intend to develop projects and feel that they need external expertise. Similarly EU operators, like hotel management groups or companies specialised in the operation of leisure and entertainment facilities, can provide services to Cambodian or Asian investors who intend to set up such facilities in Cambodia.

• Vocational training: due to the low level of education and lack of qualifications, there are opportunities for European Tourism Schools to provide training to tourism operators. ,

• Investment: EU investors can provide capital to finance tourism projects in Cambodia.

8.6 Project: "Les Portes d'Angkor"

European expertise in hotel and resort development and management would be well suited to the needs of a site like Siem Reap/Angkor. The Authority for the Protection and Management of Angkor and the Region of Siem Reap (APSARA) together with AFD (Agence Française de Développement, the French Development Agency) are promoting a project provisionally named "les Portes d'Angkor", that aims at developing a new area between the city of Siem Reap and the Angkor Wat Archaeological Park.

This well-located area, comprising about 440 ha, will include:

• cultural facilities,

• resort hotels,

• a convention centre,

• entertainment facilities such as a golf course, recreation park, etc.

The objective is to provide high quality facilities that will encourage tourists to stay longer in Siem Reap by offering a mix of culture and entertainment in a well designed and managed complex.

Substantial ground work, including the acquisition and clearance of about 100 ha of land and the building of roads has already been completed. Commitments have been made for several projects, including the building of APSARA's headquarters and a museum of Asian textiles.

9. Agro-processing

9.1 General description

Cambodia's agricultural GDP is composed of food and industrial crops (50%), fisheries (30%), livestock (14%) and forestry (6%).

Local market

Given the abundance of natural resources, Cambodia has a big potential to develop its agriculture and agro-industry. The Cambodian government, with the assistance of the international community, is promoting the development of agriculture, which is seen as the most important engine to reduce poverty in the country. Private investment, both domestic and foreign, has an important role to play in this sector.

Although progress has been achieved over the last ten years, such as in the increase of rice production yield from 1.3 to 2.1 tons per hectare, there is great potential for growth in the area of primary production, and furthermore in the area of processing.

Most Cambodian farmers grow rice, and to a smaller extent maize, on small plots of land of less than 2 ha in average. Rice and maize account for above 90% of the land used for dry seed crops. The cultivation of these crops is essentially a means of survival for farmers.

Agro-industry is only nascent. It accounts for 3.2% of GDP and provides less than 1% of total employment.

All assessments made by the government and donor agencies, including the EC, emphasise the need for agricultural diversification and agri-business. There is unanimous agreement that this represents one of the only ways of developing the country and that potential for successful investments is high.

9.2 Government policies, legal and regulatory framework

The First Socio Economic Development Plan (SEDP I –1996-2000) highlighted food security and transition to a market-based agriculture. Under SEDP II (2001-2005) the government aims to transform agriculture into an economic driving force. The strategy aims to (a) promote a consistent macroeconomic and agricultural policy framework for a liberal and market-oriented trade environment by deregulating agricultural input and output markets; (b) establish policy and legal frameworks for effective land management and administration; (c) accelerate sustainable irrigation development; (d) strengthen essential agricultural support services and (e) develop quality standards for agricultural outputs.

9.2.1 Land Law

The Land Law enacted in 2001 provides the framework for land ownership in the country and provides the legal mechanism for titling and land dispute resolution. The Law clarifies the rules regarding concessions of state land: it allows the state to grant non-transferable land concessions to private persons for up to 10 000 hectares for a maximum period of 99 years.

9.2.2 Geographical Indications

The government is drafting legislation to allow the development of a system to protect and promote the Geographical Indications of certain specific Cambodian products, in line with the TRIPS Agreement of the WTO. A GI adds value to a product as it confers special quality which derives from the product's geographical origin and entails a premium price.

9.2.3 Water Law

The government is drafting a Water Law to address the problem of insufficient irrigation infrastructure, in particular by allowing the setting up of small and medium-scale irrigation schemes by farmers' communities.

9.3 Main actors in agro-processing sector

The Cambodian agro-industrial sector consists of a large number of small and micro-enterprises with little integration among themselves and with the markets. Value chain studies (in particular recent surveys conducted by the IFC) have shown that the larger companies rely very little on small domestic firms for their inputs and supplies. Small firms typically sell their products directly to the consumers or to local traders.

The majority of the small firms are rice millers. Others process simple food products such as fish paste, smoked dried fermented or salted fish, fermented cabbage, pickled vegetables, baked goods and dried fruit.

In Phnom Penh and other main cities, there are a few larger food processing companies, like noodle manufacturers, small canneries, soy and chilli sauce makers and bottling plants. There is a lack of precise information on these firms, many of which are not registered.

There are only very few sizeable companies in the agro-industrial sector in Cambodia. The main ones are:

- **The Mong Retthy Group,** a Cambodian firm that is active in palm oil and cattle breeding, in partnership with investors from Thailand and Malaysia.

- **CP Cambodia,** the Cambodian subsidiary of the CP Group of Thailand, which is involved in feed mill and chicken farms.

- **British American Tobacco** (BAT), the international firm that is involved in a joint-venture with Cambodian partners to produce cigarettes in a factory near Phnom Penh. BAT has established a model of cooperation with more than 800 farmers by providing them with seeds, curing barns and technical assistance in agronomic practices.

- **Angkor Kasekam Rongroeung,** a Cambodian firm that owns and operates a modern rice mill in Kampong Speu province, and works on the BAT model by providing contracted farmers with seeds and technical assistance, and by assuring set prices to the farmers.

- **Huatraco pig farm,** a project set up near Phnom Penh to raise quality pigs, with technical assistance and inputs from subsidiaries of French companies based in Vietnam.

9.4 Business associations

Several sector associations are active in the agro-industrial sector, including:

- the Federation of Rice Millers Associations,
- the Spice Association,
- the Fish Processors Association,
- the Salt Producers Association.

9.5 Constraints

The development of an active agro-industrial sector is hampered by the following constraints:

- **Land issues:** the revised Land Law is meant to set out clear rules on land ownership. However establishment and granting of agricultural titles remain problematic and many disputes are reported. Currently only 10% of farmers hold legal land titles. Land concessions for agriculture are also problematic: the Ministry of Agriculture, Forestry and Fisheries (MAFF) has issued 25 land concessions for agricultural production covering about 724 000 hectares, almost 30% of cropped land. However only less than 2% of these lands have been planted, the remainder being left idle due to the lack of infrastructure

or disputes about land issues. The implementation of the new rule setting a maximum of 10000 hectares for individual land concessions should release 412000 hectares of land. The actual enforcement of this provision and the improved management of land rights will represent necessary steps that will condition investment in large-scale agriculture and downstream processing.

- **Infrastructure:** the development of crops is constrained by inadequate irrigation infrastructure. Poor roads, insufficient and expensive power, costly fuel constitute heavy impediments to the growth of agro-industries.

- **Access to quality inputs:** the access to improved seeds and other inputs such as fertilisers is still limited due to farmers' lack of information and their aversion to change.

More generally, entrepreneurs in agro-industry are constrained by the impediments that have been described earlier, for example a lack of capital and limited access to external financial support, lack of information on markets, difficult access to the markets due to insufficient means of transportation and to administrative obstacles, lack of technology and lack of skills.

9.6 Positive factors

In spite of the above-listed constraints, Cambodia's farmers and food product manufacturers manage to provide consumers with a diverse range of produce, which testifies to the traditional ability of the country and its farmers.

Being free from large polluting industries, Cambodia could develop a strategy to produce organic agricultural products. Some pilot projects for the production of such products are ongoing. The European Commission is assisting the Cambodian government to prepare an action plan to commercialise GMO-free and organic products, and a new law is being prepared to regulate the certification of these products.

9.7 Opportunities for EU companies in agro processing

The EU has a strong agro-industrial sector and major distribution companies. They can contribute to the development of Cambodia's agro-industrial sector in the following ways:

- Selling equipments, inputs and services: as Cambodian food processing companies grow in size and sophistication, there will be opportunities to supply equipment (cold storage, processing plants such as slaughter houses, fish and seafood processing equipment, packaging equipment, etc.), inputs and services (engineering, technical assistance) to the sector. One particular area of interest will be the provision of services related to the certification of the quality of food products. Another area of interest will be the provision of services, technical assistance and equipment for the production of agro bio products.

• <u>Buying products:</u> as the availability and quality of Cambodian products increase, EU distribution firms will find opportunities to diversify their sources of tropical food products. This will be the case in particular for the range of Cambodian specialty products that will benefit from the legislation on geographical indications (a provisional list includes pepper, other spices and herbs, rice, silk, etc.).

Rubber will be another product that will benefit from current initiatives of the Cambodian government, with the assistance of the French government, towards putting in place legislation and facilities to ensure the certification of high quality Cambodian rubber, in accordance with the International Rubber Association requirements. Once this is achieved, Cambodian rubber producers will be able to obtain a better price for their products.

• <u>Investment:</u> as overall conditions improve, there will be opportunities for EU companies to invest in agriculture and agro-industry in Cambodia. The improved enforcement of land concessions, in particular, will be an essential element that will allow investment in large integrated operations. In particular, the sector of cattle and poultry breeding and meat processing appears to be promising. Likewise, the sector of fisheries has a strong potential, in view of the vast resources of fish and seafood that are available in Cambodia, both in the rivers and the Tonle Sap lake and in the sea waters.

10. Infrastructure

10.1 General description

Cambodia's low income, low population density and recent history are reflected in the poor coverage, quality and efficiency of much of its infrastructure. The existing services are concentrated in the urban areas; the rural majority of the population has little access to adequate roads or other transportation means, reliable supply of electricity and safe water, and telephone connections.

Unlike most developing countries, Cambodia has acquired a significant experience in private sector participation in infrastructure (PPI). Foreign investors are involved in telecommunications and airports and a sizeable number of Cambodian entrepreneurs own and operate small power and water networks.

The recourse to private investment was motivated by the fact that public funds and donors' financial support were not sufficient to provide the required level of investment. A recent study by the World Bank has shown that government resources only cover 6% of the required investment for the 2001-2003 period, external aid being expected to provide 28%. The policy to involve the private sector also recognised the fact that it is usually an efficient provider of quality and cost effective services.

The participation of the private sector in a number of projects has been a positive development for Cambodia, and the government intends to expand the involvement of local and foreign investors in infrastructure projects. However the practice of PPI will need to improve substantially to achieve standards that will be conducive to sustained interest on the part of foreign investors.

10.2 Legal and regulatory framework for PPI projects

The legal and regulatory framework for PPI projects in Cambodia is still at an early stage of formulation and implementation. This is also true of the institutional and procedural framework. An overall law on PPI is at the drafting stage, it will take some time before it is finalised. In some sectors, like the power sector, legislation has been completed and subsequent organisational and institutional changes have been implemented. In the other sectors, laws are being drafted and institutions have not yet changed.

Cross-cutting issues affect PPI projects as they do for all investment projects. The incomplete nature of the legal system, coupled with an unclear allocation of responsibilities between levels of government and among agencies, creates costs and uncertainty for investors. The Ministry of Economy and Finance (MoEF) has in principle a key role to play in all PPI transactions, as specified in the 1993 Financial Budgetary Law that requires all PPI contracts to be approved by the MoEF. In fact, it has been bypassed in several instances.

Similarly the CDC has been designated (sub-decree 70 of July 2001) as the central agency responsible for project evaluation and inter-ministerial coordination. All BOT projects are placed under its jurisdiction. In fact, CDC's capacity to effectively fulfil its role needs to be considerably strengthened.

The judicial system also needs to become more efficient and independent in order to ensure a fair resolution of possible disputes.

Other important issues are the insufficient transparency of project planning and bidding processes, and the lack of project finance sources.

10.3 Main sectors

Under this section the sectors of power, telecommunications and water are presented. They are the main sectors where private sector participation appears to have good potential. In the transportation sector, the situation is diverse: the road sub-sector does not seem to offer attractive opportunities for the time being due to the low levels of traffic; the railway sub-sector is in a deep state of decay and would require massive investment to be brought back to an acceptable level of service. As regards the port sub-sector, the main facility at Sihanoukville is currently being expanded and upgraded with Japanese aid, which would indicate that private involvement opportunities would be limited.

10.3.1 Power

In the power sector, the 2001 Electricity Law has clarified the institutional roles, with the Ministry of Industry, Mines and Energy (MIME) as policy-maker and the newly-formed Electricity Authority of Cambodia (EAC) performing the regulatory function. Before the Law was enacted, all the contracts with independent power producers had been negotiated with the government and the state-owned electricity company, Electricité du Cambodge (EdC).

In the new system, the main actors and their roles are as follows:

- EAC is the independent regulatory body. Its duties encompass drafting of regulations in the power sector, granting licenses to operators, setting tariffs, enforcing performance standards and resolving disputes. With regard to licenses, the Law has established a new licensing framework whereby providers of generation, transmission, distribution, dispatch, wholesale, retail supply and subcontract services will be licensed by EAC, with the possibility for a single operator to obtain a "consolidated" license allowing it to perform several services. With regard to tariffs, the Law requires EAC to ensure that they allow private producers to recover their costs.

- EdC is the main electricity company in Cambodia. It was established in 1996 as a state-owned limited liability company to generate, transmit and distribute electricity throughout the country. Following the enactment of the new Electricity Law, EdC was licensed by EAC and is now involved in three main activities: generation, national transmission and distribution. It currently serves Phnom Penh and 12 provincial towns. In Phnom Penh it provides electricity from its own generators and from two foreign-owned private producers with whom it has concluded power purchase agreements (PPA). The first project, a 35 MW diesel plant, was set up by Malaysian investors (CUPL) in 1997, under a generation license issued by the Ministry of Industry, Mines and Energy (MIME) and a power purchase agreement with EdC. The second project, a 15 MW diesel plant, was set up by a Canada-USA joint-venture (Jupiter Power Cambodia) in 2000 under similar agreements with MIME and EdC.

In the provinces EdC supplies customers with power produced by a number of small independent facilities. Recently EdC has concluded a PPA with a Chinese company for the rehabilitation and operation of a 12 Mw hydroelectric facility in Kirirom.

Further, MIME has issued a tender for the selection of a private developer to implement a 180MW hydroelectric project in Kamchay under a Build-Operate-Transfer (BOT) scheme with a 30-year concession.

- In the rural areas, various private providers supply households (only about 15% of the 2 million rural households have access to electricity). Two-thirds of the supplied households receive supplies through isolated grids and the remainder through batteries. The new Electricity Law stipulates that the medium size operators must be registered companies but the small providers may be individuals.

10.3.2 Opportunities for EU companies in the power sector

Cambodia's electricity sector is expected to grow substantially over the coming years. EdC forecasts that the country's production capacity will grow from the present level of about 250 MW to about 800 MW by the year 2011. EdC alone will not be able to meet much of this requirement due to its insufficient investment capacity; therefore there are real opportunities for private operators and investors to get involved in this market.

EU companies could pursue the following opportunities:

- Providing equipment and services: a wide range of supplies will be in demand, from heavy generation equipment to materials and appliances, as well as services. The buyers will be EdC and the Cambodian and/or foreign private operators who will set up various power projects.

- Investment: there will be opportunities to invest in projects initiated by MIME/EdC, such as the recently tendered Kamchay project. It is also possible that private investors initiate and promote projects with the Cambodian authorities. Lastly, it may be envisaged, although not in the near future, that EdC could be privatized and open for foreign participation.

10.3.3 Telecommunications

Unlike in the power sector, the legal and regulatory framework for the telecommunications sector has not yet been modernized, although a new Telecommunications Law has been under preparation for some time. The new law would create a telecommunication regulatory authority, under the Ministry of Post and Telecommunications (MPTC) that would regulate the sector and grant licenses to operators.

At present, telecommunications are ruled by several pieces of legislation, the main ones being the Law on the formation of the MPTC (1996) and the sub decree on the Organization of the MPTC (1997).

In the existing system, the main actors and their roles are as follows:

The MPTC is the body responsible for providing post and telecommunication services. It is responsible for the issuance of licenses to external operators and for setting tariffs. It is also authorised to enter into partnerships with private companies.

- MPTC is the main provider of fixed line services, with a network of a capacity of 50.000 lines, 85% of which are in Phnom Penh. MPTC has about 25.000 clients. It is involved in a joint-venture with Indosat (Indonesia) in another network of about 15 000 lines in 18 provinces, which has about 8 000 clients.

- In mobile services, there are currently three companies providing services: Mobitel, the largest operator, is a partnership between MPTC, the Royal Group, a Cambodian company, and Millicom International Cellulars, a Swedish firm. It commands a 65% market share with about 350000 clients; Camshin, 100% owned by the Thai firm Shinawatra, has a 24% market share with about 130000 clients; Casacom, a partnership between Malaysian Telecoms and Samart of Thailand has a 11% market share with about 60000 clients.

Another company, Camtel, owned by the CP Group of Thailand has obtained a license but has not yet started its service. A Korean company, SK Telecom, is also reported to have obtained a license to operate another network.

- International services are provided by two gateways, one which is fully-owned by MPTC, the other one being a joint-venture between MPTC and the Royal / Millicom partnership.

- Internet services are provided by seven operators, MPTC being involved in two of them. One of the operators, Cogetel has recently been acquired by the HUOT Group, a French company.

10.3.4 Opportunities for EU companies in Telecommunications

The Cambodian telecommunications sector is growing rapidly. Mobile phone services in particular have experienced a very fast growth which has exceeded forecasts. This has been due to the inadequate coverage of fixed line networks and, conversely, to the fast expanded coverage realized by mobile operators. For instance, Mobitel has recently engaged a USD 63 million investment programme to extend its coverage to the whole of Cambodia.

EU companies can take advantage of opportunities offered by this fast growing sector:

- Providing equipment and services: ALCATEL has supplied significant amounts of equipment to MPTC and to the mobile phone operators. Other EU companies could supply a diverse range of equipment and services.

- Investment: the estimated investment requirements in the telecommunications sector are significant. For the period 2001-2003 alone, the government estimated a total of USD 44.5 million, for which there was no financing commitment from public funds or from donors. The government will therefore continue to rely on the private sector to provide most of the capital for new projects. In particular the MPTC would favour increased private participation in the development of the fixed network.

10.3.5 Water

The water sector is ruled by a loose set of legislations, the main ones being the 1996 Law on the General Status of Public Enterprises, based on which the Phnom Penh Water Supply Authority (PPWSA) was established. The government has set out a statement on water supply that defines its overall objectives and policies: the supply of water should meet local requirements, service provision should be decentralized, an independent regulator should be set up and private sector participation should be encouraged in all areas of service provision.

Unlike in the power and telecommunications sectors, there is a clear division of responsibilities between urban and rural water supply. The main actors and their roles are as follows:

- Outside Phnom Penh, the urban water supplies are operated by the Ministry of Industry, Mines and Energy (MIME). The government's policy is to establish autonomous water supply entities where possible. So far, the Sihanoukville Water Supply Authority is the only such body that has been given authority to manage its operations as a commercial enterprise.

- In other cities, the MIME runs the water supply facilities, most of which are in need of substantial repair. Due to lack of public funds, and in response to initiatives taken by the private sector, the MIME has given a number of licenses to private operators to run water systems in district towns.

In Phnom Penh the water supply network is operated by the PPWSA, under the responsibility of the Phnom Penh Municipality. The PPWSA was transformed into a publicly owned enterprise with financial and administrative autonomy in 1996.

Since 1993 a number of grants from the UN, the World Bank, the ADB and the French and Japanese governments have helped to rehabilitate the water supply system. Today about 60% of the network has been renovated. PPWSA's objectives are to complete the rehabilitation of the main network (326 km), to increase water output from 250 000 cubic metres to 320 000 cubic metres by 2005, and to improve the billing and collection rates.

10.3.6 Opportunities for EU companies in the water sector

A number of foreign companies, including some European ones, are involved in Cambodia's water sector in providing engineering services or supplying equipment. With the expected expansion of the water networks in Phnom Penh and the main provincial cities, there will be further opportunities for EU firms to compete in this market.

In terms of investment, there may be some immediate opportunities for the EU companies that are specialized in installation and management of water supply facilities and networks. In the longer term, there may be openings by way of participation in the possible privatization of the larger water utilities such as the PPWSA.

10.4 Other sectors

Information Technology
The IT sector is nascent in Cambodia. With the rapid progress of telecommunications and the growing coverage of internet services, and the increasing number of young Cambodians taking up IT studies, there is an interesting possibility that this sector will expand in a similar way as in neighbouring Vietnam.

There are a few start-up companies in Phnom Penh that are already providing IT services to European clients.

PART III

Conclusion and recommendations

• Political and economic situation: After the dramatic events of the 1975-91 period, Cambodia has found peace and relative political stability. New institutions are in place and there has been progress in their effective functioning. The economy has been improving with rather good overall GDP growth, the main problems being the excessive weight of an inefficient agriculture and a population doubled last 20 years and excessive reliance on the garment and tourism sectors, the whole system being unable to provide enough new employment and lift the country out of poverty. Structural reforms have been initiated in many areas but their effective implementation has been slow.

• The private sector environment is characterised by numerous constraints including a weak legal and judicial system, corruption, poor administration, high operating costs, competition from smuggled imported products, lack of standards and quality, scarcity of financing.

• Positive elements include Cambodia's accession to the WTO and its integration in ASEAN. Cambodia is also set to benefit from its good record in terms of social norms compliance and from the access of its exports to the EU and US markets.

• In the medium-term, Cambodia is set to benefit from improvements in infrastructure that will enhance its situation in the dynamic Mekong basin sub-region.

• With regard to potential EU-Cambodia business co-operation, there are opportunities in the provision of goods and services in several sectors. There are also opportunities to buy and distribute a range of Cambodian products. Direct investment is particularly encouraged by Cambodia's authorities. The overall investment climate, notably the legal and regulatory framework, is set to improve substantially in the near future.

ANNEXES

ANNEX 1 – Cambodia WTO Accession

Decision of 11 September 2003 + Press release

WORLD TRADE

ORGANIZATION

WT/MIN(03)/18

11 September 2003

(03-4846)

MINISTERIAL CONFERENCE
Fifth Session
Cancún, 10 - 14 September 2003

ACCESSION OF THE KINGDOM OF CAMBODIA

Decision of 11 September 2003

The Ministerial Conference,

Having regard to paragraph 2 of Article XII and paragraph 1 of Article IX of the Marrakesh Agreement Establishing the World Trade Organization (the "WTO Agreement"), and the Decision-Making Procedures under Articles IX and XII of the WTO Agreement agreed by the General Council (WT/L/93),

Taking note of the application of the Kingdom of Cambodia for accession to the WTO Agreement dated 19 October 1994,

Noting the results of the negotiations directed toward the establishment of the terms of accession of the Kingdom of Cambodia to the WTO Agreement and having prepared a Protocol on the Accession of the Kingdom of Cambodia,

Decides as follows:

1.   The Kingdom of Cambodia may accede to the WTO Agreement on the terms and conditions set out in the Protocol annexed to this Decision.

PROTOCOL ON THE ACCESSION OF THE KINGDOM OF CAMBODIA

PREAMBLE

The World Trade Organization (hereinafter referred to as the "WTO"), pursuant to Article XII of the Marrakesh Agreement Establishing the World Trade Organization (hereinafter referred to as the "WTO Agreement"), and the Kingdom of Cambodia,

Taking note of the Report of the Working Party on the Accession of the Kingdom of Cambodia to the WTO Agreement reproduced in document WT/ACC/KHM/21, dated 15 August 2003 (hereinafter referred to as the "Working Party Report"),

Having regard to the results of the negotiations on the accession of the Kingdom of Cambodia to the WTO Agreement,

Agree as follows:

PART I - GENERAL

1.   Upon entry into force of this Protocol pursuant to paragraph 8, the Kingdom of Cambodia accedes to the WTO Agreement pursuant to Article XII of that Agreement and thereby becomes a Member of the WTO.

2.   The WTO Agreement to which the Kingdom of Cambodia accedes shall be the WTO Agreement, including the Explanatory Notes to that Agreement, as rectified, amended or otherwise modified by such legal instruments as may have entered into force before the date of entry into force of this Protocol. This Protocol, which shall include the commitments referred to in paragraph 224 of the Working Party Report, shall be an integral part of the WTO Agreement.

3.   Except as otherwise provided for in paragraph 224 of the Working Party Report, those obligations in the Multilateral Trade Agreements annexed to the WTO Agreement that are to be implemented over a period of time starting with the entry into force of that Agreement shall be implemented by the Kingdom of Cambodia as if it had accepted that Agreement on the date of its entry into force.

4.   The Kingdom of Cambodia may maintain a measure inconsistent with paragraph 1 of Article II of the General Agreement on Trade in Services (hereinafter referred to as "GATS") provided that such a measure was recorded in the list of Article II Exemptions annexed to this Protocol and meets the conditions of the Annex to the GATS on Article II Exemptions.

PART II - SCHEDULES

5.   The Schedules reproduced in Annex I to this Protocol shall become the Schedule of Concessions and Commitments annexed to the General Agreement on Tariffs and Trade 1994 (hereinafter referred to as the "GATT 1994") and the Schedule of Specific Commitments annexed to the GATS relating to the Kingdom of Cambodia. The staging of the concessions and commitments listed in the Schedules shall be implemented as specified in the relevant parts of the respective Schedules.

6.   For the purpose of the reference in paragraph 6(a) of Article II of the GATT 1994 to the date of that Agreement, the applicable date in respect of the Schedules of Concessions and Commitments annexed to this Protocol shall be the date of entry into force of this Protocol.

PART III - FINAL PROVISIONS

7.   This Protocol shall be open for acceptance, by signature or otherwise, by the Kingdom of Cambodia until 31 March 2004.

8.   This Protocol shall enter into force on the thirtieth day following the day upon which it shall have been accepted by the Kingdom of Cambodia.

9.   This Protocol shall be deposited with the Director-General of the WTO. The Director-General of the WTO shall promptly furnish a certified copy of this Protocol and a notification of acceptance by the Kingdom of Cambodia thereto pursuant to paragraph 9 to each Member of the WTO and to the Kingdom of Cambodia.

This Protocol shall be registered in accordance with the provisions of Article 102 of the Charter of the United Nations.

Done at Cancún this eleventh day of September, two thousand and three in a single copy in the English, French and Spanish languages, each text being authentic, except that a Schedule annexed hereto may specify that it is authentic in only one of these languages.

ANNEX I

SCHEDULE CLVI – THE KINGDOM OF CAMBODIA

Authentic only in the English language.

(Circulated in document WT/ACC/KHM/21/Add.1)

———————

THE KINGDOM OF CAMBODIA

SCHEDULE OF SPECIFIC COMMITMENTS ON SERVICES
LIST OF ARTICLE II EXEMPTIONS

Authentic only in the English language.

(Circulated in document WT/ACC/KHM/21/Add.2)

PRESS RELEASE

PRESS/354
11 September 2003

(03-4734)

ACCESSIONS

Ambition achieved as ministers seal Cambodia membership deal

WTO ministers approved Cambodia's membership agreement today (11 September 2003), putting the Southeast Asian country in line to become the WTO's 147th member and the first least-developed country to join the WTO through the full working party negotiation process.

Cambodia still has to ratify the agreed terms and inform the WTO. Thirty days after that it will become a member. Cambodia applied to join the WTO in late 1994.

"The swift conclusion of Cambodia's membership negotiation shows that the new guidelines to allow least-developed countries to negotiate membership more easily are working," said WTO Director-General Supachai Panitchpakdi.

"It is also a signal that WTO member governments are serious in their commitment to improving developing countries' and least-developed countries' participation in the world trading system," Dr Supachai said.

Cambodia's Commerce Minister Cham Prasidh, said: "We managed to secure a package of commitments and concessions we feel was the most affordable and possible deal for Cambodia's accession, bearing in mind Cambodia's little political and economic weight and its current reliance on external assistance from the major donor countries who are also WTO members."

According to the latest WTO data, Cambodia's merchandise exports were US$1.4 billion in 2002, and its imports were US$2.0 billon.

What Cambodia has promised

Cambodia's terms of accession are spelt out in the membership agreement which consists of a report from the working party that negotiated the deal, and schedules or lists of commitments on import duties for goods and market access for service providers.

The working party took note of Cambodia's commitments, for example:

State ownership and privatization: Privatization was carried out during a first phase from 1991 to mid-1993, and a second phase starting in April 1995. Cambodia will ensure transparency, and keep WTO members informed and also provide periodic reports on other issues related to its economic reform as relevant to its obligations under the WTO.

Pricing policies: From accession, in the application of price controls, Cambodia will apply price controls in a way that is consistent with the WTO, and take account of the interests of exporting WTO members. Cambodia has published a list of goods and services subject to state control.

Trading rights (the right to import and export): Responding to a comment that its restrictions on imported pharmaceuticals and veterinary medicines could discriminate in favour of domestic production of similar products, Cambodia said that no later than 1 June 2005, it would amend its legislation, and ensure that its laws and regulations are in full conformity with its WTO obligations.

Other customs duties and charges: Cambodia will ensure these comply with WTO provisions from the date of accession and will be bound at zero.

Tariff rate quotas, tariff exemptions: Cambodia confirmed that it would respect WTO disciplines on tariff rate quotas.

Cambodia said that upon accession to the WTO, any tariff exemptions would only be implemented in conformity with the relevant WTO provisions.

Fees and charges for services rendered: All fees and charges collected for services related to imports and exports will conform with the provisions of WTO agreements, and from the date of accession, Cambodia will not apply, introduce or reintroduce any fees and charges for services rendered that were applied to imports ad valorem (i.e. as a percentage of the prices).

Application of internal taxes: From the date of accession, Cambodia will apply its domestic taxes in strict compliance with Article 3 of GATT and in a non-discriminatory manner to imports regardless of country of origin. GATT Article 3 deals with "national treatment" (or non-discrimination between locals and foreigners) in taxation.

Quantitative import restrictions, including prohibitions, quotas and licensing systems: No later than 1 June 2005, Cambodia will eliminate quantitative restrictions on imports of fertilizers, pesticides and other agricultural inputs and establish a WTO-consistent method of registration and review of imported agricultural chemicals. From 1 January 2007 Cambodia will rely on the provisions of the Technical Barriers to Trade Agreement to regulate domestic and international trade in these items.

From accession, Cambodia will not introduce, re-introduce or apply other non-tariff measures such as licensing, quotas, prohibitions, bans and other restrictions having equivalent effect that could not be justified under the provisions of the WTO Agreements.

Customs valuation: Cambodia will fully implement the Customs Valuation Agreement from 1 January 2009.

Rules of origin: Cambodia will comply fully with the provisions of the WTO Rules of Origin Agreement by 1 January 2005, parts by 1 January 2004.

Other customs formalities: A dispute settlement mechanism within the Cambodian Customs Service to handle complaints about customs practices from traders and governments will be established before 1 January 2005.

Preshipment inspection: From accession the Cambodian government will take full responsibility to ensure that the operations of the preshipment inspection companies retained by Cambodia meet the requirements of the WTO agreements. Cambodia's preshipment inspection regime will be temporary and will cease when the Customs and Excise Department is able to carry out the functions currently performed by preshipment inspection service providers.

Anti-dumping, countervailing duties, safeguard regimes: Cambodia will not apply any anti-dumping, countervailing or safeguard measure until it has notified and implemented appropriate laws and regulations conforming with the WTO agreements. After that, Cambodia will also only apply any anti-dumping duties, countervailing duties and safeguard measures in full conformity with the relevant WTO provisions.

Export restrictions: Cambodia restricts exports of rice, round logs, unprocessed timber, forestry products, antiques more than 100 years old, narcotic drugs and poisons, weapons, explosives, ammunition, and vehicles and machinery for military purposes. From the date of accession, Cambodia will ensure that restrictions comply with WTO agreements.

Export subsidies: Cambodia will comply with the Subsidies Agreement from accession. It will either eliminate the existing system of remission of import fees and waiver of duty for certain goods used by certain investors, or establish a functioning duty drawback system consistent with WTO provisions, through amendment of the Law on Investment, as necessary, by the end of 2013.

Industrial policy, including subsidies: These subsidies are to be notified from the date of accession.

Standards and certification: Cambodia will gradually implement the Technical Barriers to Trade Agreement. Full implementation will start from 1 January 2007 without recourse to any further transitional period.

Sanitary and phytosanitary measures: Cambodia will gradually implement the SPS Agreement, with full implementation by 1 January 2008. Cambodia will consult with WTO Members upon request if they deem that any measures applied during the transition period affected their trade negatively.

Trade-related investment measures (TRIMs): Cambodia will not maintain any measures inconsistent with the TRIMs Agreement and will apply the TRIMs Agreement from the date of accession without recourse to any transitional period.

State trading entities: Cambodia will apply its laws and regulations governing the trading activities of state-owned enterprises in full conformity with the provisions of the WTO Agreement.

Free zones, special economic areas: Free zones or special economic areas, including special promotion zones established in accordance with the Law on Investment, will be fully subject to the coverage of WTO agreements and its commitments in its Protocol of Accession to the WTO Agreement. Cambodia will ensure enforcement of its WTO obligations in those zones or areas. In addition, from the date of accession goods produced in these zones or areas under tax and tariff provisions that exempt imports and imported inputs from tariffs and certain taxes will be subject to normal customs formalities when entering the rest of Cambodia, including the application of tariffs and taxes.

Transit: Cambodia will apply any laws, regulations and practices governing transit operations and would act in full conformity with the provisions of the WTO agreements.

Agricultural policies: Cambodia binds its agricultural export subsidies at zero, and will not maintain or apply any export subsidies for agricultural products.

Textiles regime: Textiles and clothing import quotas that other members apply to imports from Cambodia will have growth rates applied as provided for in the Agreement on Textiles and Clothing shall be applied, from the date of Cambodia's accession. These growth rates will end when the Agreement on Textiles and Clothing terminates (in 2005).

Trade-related aspects of intellectual property rights (TRIPS): Cambodia will apply the TRIPS Agreement no later than 1 January 2007, with some protection provided in the interim.

Transparency: From the date of accession, all laws and regulations will be published according to WTO requirements, and on a website from 1 January 2004.

Regional trade agreements: Cambodia's only regional trade agreement is within ASEAN (the ASEAN Free Trade Area). In this, Cambodia will gradually eliminate tariffs on essentially all ASEAN products by 2015. Details will be notified to the WTO.

The countries that negotiated with Cambodia

Working party members: Australia, Canada, China, EU, India , Japan, Rep. Korea, Malaysia, New Zealand, Panama, Singapore, Chinese Taipei, Thailand, United States, Venezuela

Chairperson: A. Meloni (Italy)

Cambodia's Working Party was established on 21 December 1994. Cambodia submitted a Memorandum on its Foreign Trade Regime in June 1999. Replies to questions concerning the Memorandum were circulated in January 2001, the latest revisions and updates arriving in March 2003.

The 14 November 2002 meeting was the working party's third. It marked an advancement of the accession process because for the first time members focused on ideas for a draft Working Party Report and, thereby, concentrated on agreeing Cambodia's terms of entry.

The 16 April 2003 meeting was the first to consider the report. The final revision was approved at the last working party meeting on 22 July 2003.

Next

After the Cancún Ministerial Conference has approved the package, Cambodia will then have to ratify the agreement and inform the WTO. It will become a full member 30 days later.

For more information go to the WTO webiste:
Cambodia's accesion
http://www.wto.org/english/thewto_e/acc_e/a1_cambodge_e.htm
Cambodia's main page:
http://www.wto.org/english/thewto_e/countries_e/cambodia_e.htm

END

ANNEX 2 – Starting a business in Cambodia
– Information on the Council for the Development of Cambodia (CDC) –

• Screening, registration and authorisation

To start a business in Cambodia, investors have to follow administrative procedures (summarised in figure 1). The time needed to get started depends on the nature of the planned operation and the complexity of the project. In certain circumstances, an investor can start operations within a month of setting foot on Cambodian soil. However, if the investment requires the installation of additional utilities or if it is to be in a restricted are such as mining, forestry or construction that involves the authority of many government agencies, the process can take more time – six months or longer. The CDC endeavours to assist investors in obtaining permits, but more improvement in service delivery is still needed in order to reduce the time it takes investors to get their business going.

Every business in Cambodia must register with the Ministry of Commerce. An investment project must also register with the CDC before commencing operations if it wants to benefit from incentives. The registration is fairly straightforward; however, a large volume of documentation needs to be prepared (for example, the Memorandum and Articles of Association) in the Khmer language and submitted with the application form to register a business. The business also needs to register its address with City Hall. Once this is done, the business will receive a registration certificate indicating number. The process usually takes three weeks.

• Incorporation and related requirements

According to the proposed company law, the legal entities can take one of main forms: limited liability company, branch office, representative office, partnership or sole proprietorship. There are three types of limited liability companies allowable: single-member limited company, private limited company and public limited company. Limited liability companies are the entities preferred by most foreign investors setting up business in Cambodia. These companies offer the same advantages to investors as corresponding corporate bodies do in other countries. A shareholder's liability for any deficiency on winding up is usually limited to the amount unpaid for the issued and called-up shares. Shares in any company may be transferred without affecting the continuity of the business.

• Establishing a limited liability company

Company formation need not be initiated by a lawyer and is normally a simple procedure. To form a company, the founder members (subscribers) must sign the statutory documents – the Memorandum and Articles of Association – together with various other statutory forms and submit them to the Ministry of Commerce in Phnom Penh to obtain a certificate of incorporation.

A limited liability company has a minimum of 2 and a maximum of 30 shareholders. The minimum issued and paid-up capital is 20 million Riels (approximately $5,100) at a par value per share of at least 20,000 Riels. Issued capital can be either in the form of fully paid-in cash or in the form of non-cash items; however, the capital must be in place before the company can be incorporated. There is no restriction on the appointment of directors. A limited liability company is considered to have Cambodian nationality and is referred as a "local company" if it has a registered office in Cambodia and at least 51% of its shares are owned by Cambodian nationals. The chairman of the board of a local company (which can own land) must be a Cambodian national; others directors need not to be.

Figure 1: <u>STAGES OF IMPLEMENTATION OF FDI PROJECTS</u>

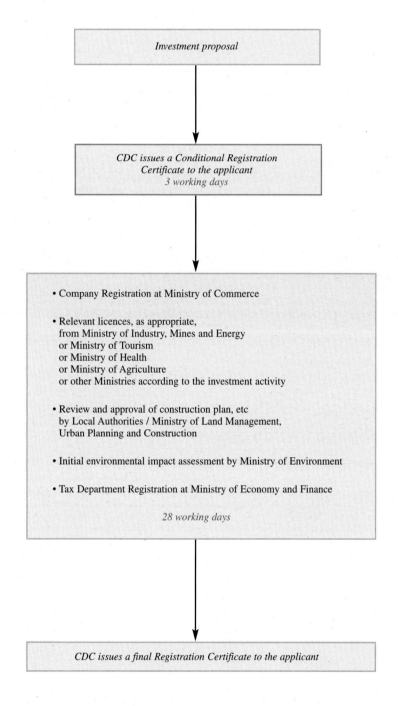

Notes

• Provided that the project is not in areas in which investment is prohibited, CDC will accept the investment proposal and proceed as above.

• Projects with certain attributes need to the Council of Ministers for approval.

• The CDC will obtain all the licences from relevant ministries or other entities listed in the Conditional Registration Certificate on behalf of the applicant. All government entities responsible for issuing authorizations, clearances, licences, permits or registrations listed on the Conditional Registration Certificate will issue such documents no later than the 25th working day from the date of the Conditional Registration Certificate.

ANNEX 3 – Sources of Information

	Study Title	Date	Author/ Editor	Address	Summary
1	Cambodia Investment Guide 2002	2002	DFDL/Mekong Law group, Lawyers &Advisers; licensed by the Council for the Developement of Cambodia	Mr Kong Chung; Ry Ouk; David Doran - 45 Preah Suramarit Blvd;POBOX 7 - Phnom Penh. Cambodia 855 23 428 726/360 545 info@dfdl.com.kh	Complete overview of the legal system in Cambodia, resume of laws, taxes, contracts and procedures; updated every year by by lawyers and legal advisers in Phnom Penh.
2	"Preparing the small and medium enterprises program"	2004	Ministry of Industry, Mines & Energy - ADB - Beijing Dyue Consulting/ Landell Mills limited, Puleu Pich consultants, Cambodia Ltd.	Draft report A D B - TA 4179	This report emphasises that the SMEs in Cambodia face a weak legal and regulatory environment which creates uncertainties and increases the risk of doing business. The final section explains the proposed reform policy agenda.
3	Implementing the Integrated Framework "IF" in Cambodia	2002	Ministry of Commerce (WTO,WB,ITC,UNCTAD, IMF, UNDP)	Ministry of Commerce Royal Government of Cambodia - Phnom Penh - Cham Prasidh Minister of Commerce	Overview of the collaborative efforts to promote an integrated approach to Trade Assistance and elaboration of the Trade Strategy; TA Matrix (p31) (priorities/- private sectors); bi-lateral and multi lateral partnerships; trade capacity building; examples of initiatives and projects.
4	Cambodia: Seizing the Global Opportunity - Investment climate and reform strategy for Cambodia	2004	World Bank Group for Royal Cambodian Government	21/0	The report gives figures and data and factors of productivity in Cambodia. It employs an investment climate survey of 800 formal and informal firms, and benchmarks the response with with those of China, Bangladesh, India & Pakistan. It was prepared to help the stakeholders identify and prioritise policy reforms in economy and business environment.
5	Cambodia Investment Potential - Challenge and Prospects	2003	Japan international co-operation agency		Guidelines presented as investment information to policy makers and to academia interested in Cambodia's potential - Detailed statistics for researchers. Project of Law on Investment amendement (p73).
6	The joint development study for **economic cooperation** plan between **Thailand and Cambodia**	2001	Office of the national and economic and social developement board and university research & development institute and Cambodian TCJDS Expert Group		Study to prepare the Thailand-Cambodian atrategic cooperation showing spatial settlements and prospective plans (maps) and some examples of investment potentials (energy, tourism, fisheries and projects areas with detailed budgets).

7	The study on Regional Development of the **Phnom Penh-Sihanoukville growth corridor** in the Kingdom of Cambodia	Apr-03	Japan international co-operation agency	Nippon Koei/IDCG/KRI international	Regional development study giving details of SPZ project (Special Promotion Zone) and slides of Speakers of the 5th Workshop of the Jica Growth Corridor Development Study of April 2003.
8	Studies on the rural investment carried out in 2001 for the technical coordination office of the C in Cambodia (Mission in Malaysia, Thailand, Vietnam, Recommendations)	Not available			
9	Report on the workshop on the assessment of the **agro-industrial** situation in Cambodia	2003	PRASAC II European Commission	Martin Gummert - Consultant	Complete and detailed market study and of agricultural production and demand, and agro industry. Example of Village Pilot testing projects (drying high value, electicity generation, oil extraction, feed mills) and a list of agro-based companies established in Cambodia.
10	UNDP Asia Trade Initiative- Country study on Trade in Textiles and Clothing	Aug-03	UNDP	project RAS/01/060-SSA03-02730	Market analysis with sectorial views including future of Asia IT&C industries, figures and trade flows, domestic strategies.
11	L'industrie de la confection au Cambodge	May-03	Mission économique de Phnom Penh	DREE. French Ministry of Economy and Finance- 1 Bld Monivong- Phnom Penh - Cambodia.	Synthetic Market survey offering sectorial views, figures, graphs, facts and major events and actors' prospectives
12	Le marché des fruits et légumes au Cambodge	Jun-03	Mission économique de Phnom Penh	DREE. French Ministry of Economy and Finance- 1 Bld Monivong- Phnom Penh - Cambodia.	Synthetic market survey offering sectorial views, figures, graphs, facts and major events and actors' prospectives.
13	Le marché des produits carnés au Cambodge	Jun-03	Mission économique de Phnom Penh	DREE. French Ministry of Economy and Finance- 1 Bld Monivong- Phnom Penh - Cambodia.	Synthetic Market survey offering sectorial views, figures, graphs, facts and major events and actors' prospectives.
14	Le caoutchouc au Cambodge	May-03	Mission économique de Phnom Penh	DREE. French Ministry of Economy and Finance- 1 Bld Monivong- Phnom Penh - Cambodia.	Synthetic Market survey offering sectorial views, figures, graphs, facts and major events and actors' prospectives.
15	L'élevage au Cambodge	Jun-03	Mission économique de Phnom Penh	DREE. French Ministry of Economy and Finance- 1 Bld Monivong- Phnom Penh - Cambodia.	Synthetic Market survey offering sectorial views, figures, graphs, facts and major events and actors' prospectives.
16	Matériel agricole, pesticides et angrais au Cambodge	Jul-03	Mission économique de Phnom Penh	DREE. French Ministry of Economy and Finance- 1 Bld Monivong- Phnom Penh - Cambodia.	Synthetic Market survey offering sectorial views, figures, graphs, facts and major events and actors' prospectives.
17	Le marché des boissons alcoolisées au Cambodge (June 2003)	Jun-03	Mission économique de Phnom Penh	DREE. French Ministry of Economy and Finance- 1 Bld Monivong- Phnom Penh - Cambodia.	Synthetic Market survey offering sectorial views, figures, graphs, facts and major events and actors' prospectives.

18	Le marché des produits laitiers - mai 2003	May-03	Mission economique de Phnom Penh	DREE. French Ministry of Economy and Finance- 1 Bld Monivong- Phnom Penh - Cambodia.	Synthetic Market survey offering sectorial views, figures, graphs, facts and major events and actors' prospectives.
19	La filière blé, boulangerie, patisserie au Cambodge (May 2003)	May-03	Mission economique de Phnom Penh	DREE. French Ministry of Economy and Finance- 1 Bld Monivong- Phnom Penh - Cambodia.	Synthetic Market survey offering sectorial views, figures, graphs, facts and major events and actors' prospectives.
20	Matériaux de construction (April 2003)	Apr-03	Mission economique de Phnom Penh	DREE. French Ministry of Economy and Finance- 1 Bld Monivong- Phnom Penh - Cambodia.	Synthetic Market survey offering sectorial views, figures, graphs, facts and major events and actors' prospectives.
21	Le second œuvre du bâtiment (June 2003)	Jun-03	Mission economique de Phnom Penh	DREE. French Ministry of Economy and Finance- 1 Bld Monivong- Phnom Penh - Cambodia.	Synthetic Market survey offering sectorial views, figures, graphs, facts and major events and actors' prospectives.
22	Les grands projets dans le secteur de l'eau au Cambodge	Jun-03	Mission economique de Phnom Penh	DREE. French Ministry of Economy and Finance- 1 Bld Monivong- Phnom Penh - Cambodia.	Synthetic Market survey offering sectorial views, figures, graphs, facts and major events and actors' prospectives.
23	Les transports maritimes et fluviaux au Cambodge	Feb-03	Mission economique de Phnom Penh	DREE. French Ministry of Economy and Finance- 1 Bld Monivong- Phnom Penh - Cambodia.	Synthetic Market survey offering sectorial views, figures, graphs, facts and major events and actors' prospectives.
24	Le marché du matériel bureautique et informatique au Cambodge	Jun-03	Mission economique de Phnom Penh	DREE. French Ministry of Economy and Finance- 1 Bld Monivong- Phnom Penh - Cambodia.	Synthetic Market survey offering sectorial views, figures, graphs, facts and major events and actors' prospectives.
25	Les télécommunications au Cambodge	Jun-03	Mission economique de Phnom Penh	DREE. French Ministry of Economy and Finance- 1 Bld Monivong- Phnom Penh - Cambodia.	Synthetic Market survey offering sectorial views, figures, graphs, facts and major events and actors' prospectives.
26	L'internet au Cambodge	Aug-03	Mission economique de Phnom Penh	DREE. French Ministry of Economy and Finance- 1 Bld Monivong- Phnom Penh - Cambodia.	Synthetic Market survey offering sectorial views, figures, graphs, facts and major events and actors' prospectives.
27	L'industrie de la chaussure au Cambodge	Jun-03	Mission economique de Phnom Penh	DREE. French Ministry of Economy and Finance- 1 Bld Monivong- Phnom Penh - Cambodia.	Synthetic Market survey offering sectorial views, figures, graphs, facts and major events and actors' prospectives.
28	Le marché de la lunetterie et l'optique au Cambodge	Feb-02	Mission economique de Phnom Penh	DREE. French Ministry of Economy and Finance- 1 Bld Monivong- Phnom Penh - Cambodia.	Synthetic Market survey offering sectorial views, figures, graphs, facts and major events and actors' prospectives.
29	Le marché des produits cosmétiques au Cambodge	Apr-03	Mission economique de Phnom Penh	DREE. French Ministry of Economy and Finance- 1 Bld Monivong- Phnom Penh - Cambodia.	Synthetic Market survey offering sectorial views, figures, graphs, facts and major events and actors' prospectives.
30	Le sujet de Santé au Cambodge	Aug-03	Mission economique de Phnom Penh	DREE. French Ministry of Economy and Finance- 1 Bld Monivong- Phnom Penh - Cambodia.	Synthetic Market survey offering sectorial views, figures, graphs, facts and major events and actors' prospectives.

31	Le marché des produits pharmaceutiques	Jan-02	Mission économique de Phnom Penh	DREE. French Ministry of Economy and Finance-1 Bld Monivong-Phnom Penh - Cambodia.	Synthetic Market survey offering sectorial views, figures, graphs, facts and major events and actors' prospectives.
32	Le pétrole et le gaz	Agu-03	Mission économique de Phnom Penh	DREE. French Ministry of Economy and Finance-1 Bld Monivong-Phnom Penh - Cambodia.	Synthetic Market survey offering sectorial views, figures, graphs, facts and major events and actors' prospectives.
33	Le marché des pompes et robinetterie industrielle au Cambodge	Feb-01	Mission économique de Phnom Penh	DREE. French Ministry of Economy and Finance-1 Bld Monivong-Phnom Penh - Cambodia.	Synthetic Market survey offering sectorial views, figures, graphs, facts and major events and actors' prospectives.
34	La distribution (alimentaire/ Grande distribution/ grossistes)	Jun-03	Mission économique de Phnom Penh	DREE. French Ministry of Economy and Finance-1 Bld Monivong-Phnom Penh - Cambodia.	Synthetic Market survey offering sectorial views, figures, graphs, facts and major events and actors' prospectives
35	Le secteur bancaire au Cambodge	Feb-02	Mission économique de Phnom Penh	DREE. French Ministry of Economy and Finance-1 Bld Monivong-Phnom Penh - Cambodia.	Synthetic Market survey offering sectorial views, figures, graphs, facts and major events and actors' prospectives.
36	A guide to investing in Cambodia	2000	Council for the development of Cambodia-Cambodian Investment Board	DREE. French Ministry of Economy and Finance-1 Bld Monivong-Phnom Penh - Cambodia.	Synthetic Market survey offering sectorial views, figures, graphs, facts and major events and actors' prospectives.
37	Law & regulations on investment in the Kingdom of Cambodia - Law on Investment 4/08/1994 (unofficial translation)	Not dated	Council for the development of Cambodia- CDC	Cambodian Investment Board (Department of legal affairs)-Phnom Penh	Small brochure giving unofficial translations of law on Investments and sub-degrees N°51,48,88,53.
38	Macro economic Datas	Sep-03	Cambodian Embassy in Paris	Ambassade Royale du Cambodge, 4 rue AdoplpheYvon 75116 Paris +33 01 45 08 47 19	General country figures.
39	List of 114 French enterprises situated in Cambodia	Not dated (2001 or 2002)	Cambodian Embassy in Paris	Ambassade Royale du Cambodge, 4 rue AdoplpheYvon 75116 Paris +33 01 45 08 47 20	List of 114 organisations: name, address in Cambodia, email and list of economic sectors favourable for investment (2003).
40	UNCTAD-ICC "Near final draft : An investment Guide to Cambodia-Opportunities and conditions"	Oct-03	UNCTAD- United Nations 2003	UNCTAD Palais des Nations 8-14, Av. de la Paix 1211 Geneva 10 - Switzerland T: +41 22 907 1234 F: +41 22 907 0043 info@unctad.org	General overview of Cambodia's economy for investors who are unfamiliar with the country. It offers a description of the environment and general conditions in which investors could operate. It does not constitute an exhaustive overview or provide detailed and pratical instructions. It proposes a list of major foreign investors and a comparison of FDI in ASEAN countries, and a SWOT (light) analysis if Investment Climate in Cambodia (p41).
41	Survey on the attitudes of European Business to internatioanl investments rules	Mar-00	EC DG Trade- SOFRES consultants	TN Sofres SA - Paris - France +33 01 40 92 46 67 Isabelle Sordel & Jean-Michel Perigois	

42	Unemployment in Est Asia and Europe	1999-2003	FRI Centre Asie French Independant Research institute		Report of the Council For Asia-Europe Cooperation (CAEC) + China, Japan, ASEAN: strategic competition or co-operation?
43	WTO Legal Framework	Jul-03	WTO publications news	www.wto.org	List of Cambodia commitments and promises in accession package to join WTO
44	National case study on environmental requirement in key markets for the FOOTWEAR industry	Aug-03	UNCTAD- United Nations 2003		Complete survey on criteria set by the EU market (EU eco label - France and Germany) for Cambodian footwear exports and analysis of global trends for this sector, the need for capacity building and benchmarking; transport & import clearance charges for Cambodia and 4 other countries (p41)
45	IMF CAMBODIA selected issues and statistical appendix 2003 (90 pages)	Mar-03	IMF International monetary fund	Publication services 700 19th Street N.W. WASHINGTON ,DC 20431 Tel (202) 623 7430/Fx 623 7201 www.imf.org	Complete economic key figures and reforms ratios, and statistics (evolution 5 or 10 years).
46	Projects and loans concerning Cambodia ex: Building vital road link in Cambodia for economic cooperation in Mekong subregion	2002/2003	Asian Development Bank	Manilla - Philippines www.ADB.org	ADB projects accessible by country.
47	Gavroche Reportage GENERAL PRESS REVIEW on Cambodia events	2002/2003	Francophone magazine, for Thailand, Laos, Cambodia	Bangkok - Thailand	Press review on Cambodian events.
48	Le tourisme au Cambodge	Apr-03	Mission économique de Phnom Penh	DREE. French Ministry of Economy and Finance- 1 Bld Monivong- Phnom Penh - Cambodia	General statistics; hotel/guest house and restaurant market; travel agencies, development previsions.
49	Le marché de l'assurance au Cambodge	Sep-03	Mission économique de Phnom Penh	DREE. French Ministry of Economy and Finance- 1 Bld Monivong- Phnom Penh - Cambodia.	Laws and framework market previsions.
51	Country commercial guide	2002	American Embassy	www.usembassy.state.gov/ posts/cb1/wwwh0017.html	Effcient guide to investors specifying export and investment sectors and FDI origins.

ANNEX 4 – General Information on Cambodia

GEOGRAPHY OF CAMBODIA

Data	Figures	Comments
Location	Southeastern Asia, bordering the Gulf of Thailand, between Thailand, Vietnam and Laos	Cambodia is surrounded by 3 neighbours and belongs to the greater Mekong Sub region (Laos, Myanmar, Thailand Vietnam and Yunnan Province of China)
Geographic coordinates	13 00 N, 105 00 E	
Map references	South-east Asia	
Area and Land	*Total:* 181,040 sq km *Land:* 176,520 sq km *Water:* 4,520 sq km	
• **Coastline**	443 km	
• **Terrain**	Mostly low, flat plains, mountains in southwest and north	
• **Land use**	*Arable land:* 20.96% *Permanent crops:* 0.61% *Other:* 78.43% (1998 est. include.Forest 45%)	
• **Irrigated land**	2,700 sq km (1998 est.)	
• **Geography - note**	A land of paddies and forests dominated by the Mekong River and Tonle Sap lake	
Area comparative	Twice Portugal or half Germany	
Land boundaries	*Total:* 2,572 km	
Maritime claims	*Contiguous zone:* 24 NM *Territorial sea:* 12 NM *Continental shelf:* 200 NM *Exclusive economic zone:* 200 NM	
Climate	Tropical; rainy, monsoon season (May to November); dry season (December to April); little seasonal temperature variation	
Evaluation extremes	*Lowest point:* Gulf of Thailand 0 m *Highest point:* Phnum Aoral 1,810 m	
Natural Resources	Timber, gemstones, some iron ore, manganese, phosphates, hydropower potential, oil and gas potential	
Natural hazards	Monsoonal rains (June to November): flooding; occasional droughts	
Environment-current issues	Illegal logging activities throughout the country and strip mining for gems in western region along the border with Thailand have resulted in habitat loss and declining biodiversity (in particular, destruction of mangrove swanps threat natural fisheries); soil erosion.	
Environment-international agreements	*Party to:* Biodiversity, Climate change, Desertification, Endangered Species Hazardous Wastes, Marine Life Conservation, Ozone Layer Protection, Ship Pollution, Tropical Timber 94, Wetlands *Signed, but not ratified:* Law of the Sea, Marine Dumping	As a Least Developed Country (LDC) Cambodia is furthermore entitled to benefit from the most favourable treatment under the GSP, the so-called "Everything But Arms – EBA" provisions.

PEOPLE IN CAMBODIA

Sources: ....CIA

Data	Figures	Comments	History
Population	13,124,764 *note* AIDS can result in lower life expectancy, higher infant mortality death rates, lower population and growth rates, and changes in the distribution population by age and sex than would otherwise be expected (July 2003 est.)	Estimates take into account the effects of excess mortality due to AIDS	Population Khmer and Buddhist with a large majority 90%
Age structure	*0-14 years:* 39.3% *15-64 years:* 57.6% *65 years and over:* 3.1%	(male 2,606,568; female 2,557,736) (male 3,599,216; female 3,962,520) (male 148,287; female 250,437) (2003 est.)	2 to 3 million adults were killed between 1975 and 1980
Median age	*Total:* 19.2 years	*Male:* 18.4 years *Female:* 20 years	(2002)
Population growth rate	1.8%	(2003 est.)	
Birth rate	27.28 births/ 1,000 population	(2003 est.)	
Death rate	9.26 deaths/ 1,000 population	(2003 est.)	
Net migration rate	0 migrant(s)/1,000 population	(2003 est.)	
Sex ratio	*At birth:* 1.05 male(s)/female *Under 15 years:* 1.02 male(s)/female *15-64 years:* 0.91 male(s)/female *65 years and over:* 0.59 male(s)/female	*total population:* 0.94 male(s)/female (2003 est.)	
Infant mortality rate	*Total:* 75.94 deaths/1,000 live births *Female:* 66.51 deaths/1,000 live births *Male:* 84.96 deaths/1,000 live births	(2003 est.)	
Life expectancy at birth	*Total population:* 57.92 years *Male:* 55.49 years *Female:* 60.47 years	(2003 est.)	
Total fertility rate	3.58 children born/woman	(2003 est.)	
HIV/AIDS – Adult prevalence rate	2.7%	(2001 est.)	
HIV/AIDS – people living with HIV/AIDS	170,000	(2001 est.)	
HIV/AIDS – deaths	12,000	(2001 est.)	
Nationality	*Noun:* Cambodian(s) *Adjective:* Cambodian		
Ethnic groups	Khmer 90%, Vietnamese 5%, Chinese 1%, other 4%		
Religions	Tehravada Buddhist 95%, other 5%		
Languages	Khmer (official) 95%, French, English		
Literacy	*Definition:* age 15 and over can read and write *Total population:* 69.9%	*Male:* 80.5% *Female:* 60.3% (2003 est.)	Skilled and educated people have been killed or escaped to survive under the Khmer Rouge

GOVERNMENT OF CAMBODIA

Data	Figures	Comments
Country name	*Conventional short form:* Cambodia *Local short form:* Kampuchea *Former:* Khmer Republic, Kampuchea Republic	*Conventional long form:* Kingdom of Cambodia *Local long form:* Preahreachenachakr Kampuchea
Government type	Multiparty democracy under a constitutional monarchy established in September 1993	
Capital	Phnom Penh	
Administrative divisions	Banteay Mean Cheay, Batdambang, Kampong Cham, Kampong Chnang, Kampong,Spoe, Kampong Thum, Kampot, Kandal, Kaoh Kong, Keb, Kracheh, Mondol Kiri, Otdar Mean Cheay, Pailin, Phnum Penh, Pouthisa, Preah Seihanu, Preah Vihear, Prey Veng, Rotanah Kiri, Siem Reab, Stoeng Treng, Svay Rieng, Takev	20 provinces (khett, singular and plural) and 4 municipalities (krong, singular and plural);
Independence	9 November 1953 (from France)	
National holiday	Independence Day, 9 November	
Constitution	Promulgated on 21 September 1993	
Legal system	Primarily a civil law mixture of French-influenced codes from the United Nations Transitional Authority in Cambodia (UNTAC) period, royal decrees, and acts of the legislature, with influences of customary law and remnants of communist legal theory	Increasing influence of common law in recent years
Suffrage	18 years of age; universal	
Executive branch	*Chief of state:* King Norodom SIHAMUNI *Head of government:* Prime Minister HUN SEN *Cabinet:* Council of Ministers appointed by the King Following legislative elections, a member of the majority party coalition is named Prime Minister by the chairman of the National Assembly and appointed by the King	The King is chosen by a Royal Throne council. The Government ("Royal Government of Cambodia") is formed by a vote of confidence by a two-thirds majority of the National Assembly. It is in charge of overall execution of national policies and programmes, and is accountable to the National Assembly. The Government is led by a prime minister, assisted by two deputy prime ministers, senior ministers, ministers and secretaries of state
Legislative branch	Bicameral consists of the National Assembly (122 seats; members elected by popular vote to serve five-year terms) and the Senate (61 seats; two member appointed by the monarch, two elected by the National Assembly, and 57 elected by "functional constituencies"; members serve five-year terms) *Election results:* National Assembly – percent of vote by party – CPP 41%, FUNCIPEC 32%, SRP 14%, other 13%; seats by party – CPP 64, FUNCINPEC 43, SRP 15; Senate - percent of vote by party - NA%; seats by party - CPP 31, FUNCINPEC 21, SRP 7, other 2	*Elections:* National Assembly – The last election, held in July 2003, did not give the required majority to the main party, the CPP, to allow it to form a government. A new government was formed in July 2004. Senate – last held on 2 March 1999
Juridical branch	Supreme Council of the Magistracy (provided for in the constitution and formed in December 1997); Supreme Court (and lower courts) exercises judicial authority.	
Political parties and leaders	Buddhist Liberal Party or BLP [IENG MOULY]; Cambodian Pracheachon or Cambodia People's Party or CPP [CHEA SIM]; Khmer Citizen Party or [NGUON SOEUR]; National United Front an Independent, Neutral, Peaceful, and Cooperative Cambodia or FUNCINPEC [Prince NORODOM RANARIDDH]; Sam Rangsi Party or SRP (formerly Khmer Nation ¨Party or KNP) [SAM RANGSI]	Main parties: – Cambodia People's Party or CPP – Cooperative Cambodia or FUNCINPEC – Sam Rangsi Party or SRP

Political pressure groups and leaders	Not applicable	
Membership in international organisations	ACCT, ARF, ADB, ASEAN, CP, ESCAP, FAO, G-77, IAEA, IBRD, ICAO, ICCT, ICRM, IDA, IFAD, IFC, IFRCS, ILO, IMF, IMO, Interpol, IOC, IOM, ISO (subscriber), ITU, NAM, OPCW (signatory), PCA, UN, UNCTAD, UNESCO, UNIDO, UPU, WCO, WFTU, WHO, WIPO, WMO, WTO	
Diplomatic representation in the EU	*Main Embassy in Europe:* 4 rue Adolphe Yvon 75116 Paris, France Telephone: +33 145 03 47 20 Fax: + 33 1 45 03 47 40	
Diplomatic representation from the EU	EC Delegation in Cambodia No 1, Street 21 , Phnom Penh Telephone: 023 220 611 Fax: 023 216 997 Chief of mission: Mr Winston McColgan	
Flag description	Three horizontal bands of blue (top), red (double width), and blue with a white three-towered temple representing Angkor Wat outlined in black in the center of the red band	

ECONOMY IN CAMBODIA

Data	Figures	Comments
Overview	Cambodia's economy has grown at an average rate of 6,5% from 1998 to 2002, based mainly on the expansion of the tourism and garment sectors. Macro-economic stability has been maintained with inflation kept below 4%. External debt service stands at about 3% of exports. However the economy remains fragile and growth has had a mimnimum impact on reducatyion of poverty. Cambodia's long-term development depends on improving infrastructure, education and productive skills, and attracting foreign investment.	In 1994-1995, economic growth was strong, achieving the government's target of 7 to 8%. It generated substantial employment and revenues. In 1997-1998, renewed political tensions combined with the regional financial crisis, led to a growth slowdown.
GDP	$ 3 billion	At market price, 2002 current
GDP – real growth rate	5.2%	(2002 est.)
GDP – per capita	Purchasing power parity - $1,500	(2002 est.)
GDP – composition by sector	*Agriculture:* 32% *Industry:* 24% *Services:* 43%	(2001 est. from Ministry Economy & Finance)
Population below poverty line	36% (1997 est.)	
Household income or consumption by percentage share	*Lowest 10%:* 2.9% *Highest 10%:* 33.8% (1997)	
Distribution of family income – Gini index	40.4 (1997)	
Inflation rate (consumer prices)	3.8% (2001) 3.3% (2002 est.)	
Labour force	6 million (1998 est.)	
Labour force – by occupation	Agriculture 80% (2001 est.)	
Unemployment rate	2.8% (1999 est.)	This figure should be treated with care, as many Cambodians work in the informal economy. Cambodia's private sector predominantly consists of small-scale unregistered enterprises involved in agriculture, food processing and services. This informal sector accounts for 80% of GDP and 95% of employment.
Budget	*Revenues:* $396 million *Expenditures:* $607 million, including capital *Expenditures* of $254 million (2001 est.)	
Main sectors of economic activity	Tourism, garments, rice milling, fishing, wood and wood products, rubber, gem mining	
Industrial production growth rate	16% (2001 est.), primarily in the garment sector	
Electricity – production	119 million kWh (2001)	
Electricity production by source	*Fossil fuel:* 65% *Hydro:* 35% *Other:* 0% (2001) *Nuclear:* 0%	
Electricity – consumption	110.6 million kWh (2001)	
Electricity exports	0 kWh (2001)	
Electricity imports	0 kWh (2001)	
Oil production	O bbl/day (2001 est.)	
Oil consumption	3,600 bb/day (2001 est.)	
Oil exports	Not applicable	
Oil imports	Not applicable	
Agriculture products	Rice, rubber, corn, fruits & vegetables	
Exports	$1.57 billion (2003 est.)	$1.77 billion (2002 est.)

ECONOMY IN CAMBODIA

Data	Figures	Comments
Exports commodities	Garments, rubber, rice, fish, timber	
Exports partners	US 61.5%, Germany 9.0%, UK 7.2%, Singapore 4.5%, Japan 3.8%, France 3% (2002)	
Imports	$2.4 billion (2003 est.)	$2.3 billion (2002 est.)
Imports – commodities	Petroleum products, textiles, cigarettes, gold, construction materials, machinery, motor vehicles	
Imports - partners	Thailand 30.2%, Singapore 21.5%, Hong Kong 10.2%, China 7.8%, Vietnam 6.6%, Taiwan 4.7% (2002)	
Debt – external	$829 million (1999 est.)	
Economic aid – recipient	$548 million pledged in grants and concessional loans for 2001 by international donors	
Currency	Riel (KHR)	
Currency code	KHR	
Exchange rates	Riels per US dollar – 4,070 (2004)	
Fiscal year	Calendar year	

COMMUNICATIONS IN CAMBODIA

Data	Figures	Comments
Telephones – main lines in use	100,000 (est 2000)	
Telephones – mobile cellular	80,000 (2000)- 350 000 (2003)	*Operators:* Mobitel, Camshin, Casacom
Telephone system	*General assessment:* adequate landline and/or cellular service in Phnom Penh and other provincial cities; rural areas have little telephone service *Domestic:* NA *International:* adequate but expensive landline and cellular service available to all countries from Phnom Penh and major provincial cities; satellite earth station - 1 Intersputnik (Indian Ocean region)	
Radio broadcast stations	AM 7, FM 3 shortware 3 (1999)	
Television broadcast stations	6 (2003)	
Internet country code	.kh	
Internet Service Providers (ISPs)	2 (2000) – 7 (2004)	
Internet users	10,000 (2002)	

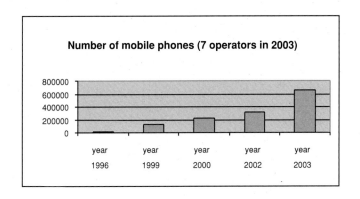

TRANSPORTATION IN CAMBODIA

Data	Figures	Comments
Railways	*Total:* 602 km *Narrow gauge:* 602 km 1.000-m gauge (2002)	
Highways	*Total:* 35,769 km *Paved:* 4,165 km *Unpaved:* 31,604 km (1997)	
Waterways	3,700 km	*note:* navigable all year to craft drawing 0.6 m or less; 282 km navigable to drawing as much as 1.8 m
Ports and harbors	Kampong Saom (Sihanoukville), Kampot, Krong Kaoh Kong, Phnom Penh	
Merchant marine	*Total:* 527 ships (1,000 GRT or over) 2,328,371 GRT/3,294,028 DWT *Ships by type:* bulk 49, cargo 412, chemical tanker 2, combination bulk 4, container 17, liquefied gas 1, livestock carrier 2, multi-functional large-load carrier 1, passenger/cargo 1, petroleum tanker 18, refrigerated cargo 11, roll on/roll off 7, short-sea passenger 2	*Note:* includes some foreign-owned ships registered here as a flag of convenience: Aruba 1, Belize 8, British Virgin Islands 1, Bulgaria 3, China Cyprus 15, Denmark 1, Egypt 7, Estonia 1, Georgia 1, Germany 1, Greece 1, Honduras 5, Hong Kong 12, Iceland 1, Indonesia 2, Iran 1, Ireland 1, Italy 1, Japan 5, Jordan 1, Latvia 2, Lebanon 5, Liberia 5, Lithuania 1, Malta 1, Netherlands 1, Norway 2, Panama 7, Romania 4, Russia 67, Saint Kitts and Nevis 10, Saint Vincent and the Grenadines 4, Singapore 15, South Korea 2, Syria 13, Thailand 1, Turkey 22, Urkiane 13, UAE 2, UK 1, US 5, Vietnam 2, Virgin Islands (UK) 1 (2002 est.)
Main airports	International airports: Phnom Penh, Siem Reap, Sihanoukville. Domestic: Battambang, Mondulkiri, Rattanakiri, Stung Treng.	
Airports – with paved runways	*Total:* 5 *2,438 to 3,047 m:* 2 *1,524 to 2,437 m:* 2 *914 to 1,523 m:* 1 (2002)	
Airports – with unpaved runways	*Total:* 16 *Under 914m:* 1 (2002) *1,524 to 2,437m:* 2 *914 to 1,523 m:* 13	
Heliports	2 (2002)	

INTERNATIONAL RELATIONS WITH CAMBODIA

Data	Figures	Comments	History
WTO	The WTO Ministerial Conference in Cancun (September 2003) approved Cambodia's accession to the WTO. The Protocol of Accession was approved by the National Assembly and the Senate in September 2004. Cambodia became a full member of WTO in October 2004.		The WTO Ministerial Conference in Cancun (September 2003) approved Cambodia's accession to the WTO.
ASEAN	Cambodia joined the Association of Southeast Asian Nations in 1999. ASEAN is composed of 10 coutries: Brunei, Cambodia, Indonesia, Lao PDR, Malaysia, Myanmar, Philippines, Singapore, Thailand, Viet Nam.		Cambodia joined the Association of Southeast Asian Nations in 1999. ASEAN is composed of 10 countries: Brunei, Cambodia, Indonesia, Lao PDR, Malaysia, Myanmar, Philippines, Singapore, Thailand, Viet Nam.
REGIONAL COOPERATION	Cambodia belongs to the Greater Mekong Sub-region (GMS), a regional cooperation programme involving Laos, Myanmar, Thailand, Vietnam and the Yunnan province of China. Thailand, Myanmar, Laos and Cambodia declared a strategy for economic cooperation in August 2003.		The GMS programme, launched in 1992 with the support of the Asian Development Bank, mainly aims at developing infra-structure projects that will greatly enhance the overall economic growth of the region.
EUROPE	Council Decision of 11 November 2002 extending and amending Decision 1999/730/CFSP concerning a European Union contribution to combating the destabilising accumulation and spread of small arms and light weapons in Cambodia		
Disputes - international	Completed boundary demarcation with Thailand; accuses Vietnam of moving and destroying boundary markers and encroachments, initiating border incidents; accuses Thailand of preventing access to Preah Vihear temple ruins awarded to Cambodia by ICJ decision in 1962; maritime boundary with Vietnam hampered by dispute over offshore islands		
Illicite drugs	Narcotics-related corruption reportedly involving some in the government, military, and police; possible small(scale opium, heroin, and amphetamine production ; large producer of cannabis for the international market ; vulnerable money laundering due to its cash-based economy and porous borders		

ANNEX 5a – Foreign and Major Enterprises in Cambodia (187)

Australian Enterprises

INDOCHINA RESEARCH LIMITED
Marketing research & consultancy services

British Enterprises

MIGHTI-SPECTRA KNITTING FACTORY CO. LTD
Knitting

WING TAI APPAREL (CAMBODIA) LTD
Garments

Cambodian Enterprises (major enterprises)

CAMBODIA MEKONG BANK PUBLIC LIMITED
Banking services

CAMGSM/MOBITEL
Telecommunications

CAMINCO
General Insurance Services

CANADIA BANK LTD. CAMBODIA
Banking

HOTEL INTERCONTINENTAL PHNOM PENH
Hotel

KONG HONG GARMENT CO. LTD
Garments

MONG RETHTHY INVESTMENT CAMBODIA
Palm Oil Plantation

TTY CO. LTD
Crumb rubber, tapioca mill, granite and saw mills

Chinese Enterprises

CAMBODIA HAINING GROUP CO. LTD
Agriculture

SABRINA GARMENT MANUFACTURING CORP.
Garments

SHANDONG DEMIAN GROUP TEXTILE CO. LTD
Textile

SU TONG FANG GROUP YING KAN GARMENT
Garments

UNIVERSAL APPAREL CO. LTD
Garments

French Enterprises (114)

ADCOMS CONSULTANTS CO.LTD
Consultant

AEA INTERNATIONAL SOS MEDICAL CENTER
Medical

AGE INTERNATIONAL AIRPORT GROUND EQUIPMENT
INTERNATIONAL LTD
Aeronautical

AGRISUD CAMBODGE

AIR FRANCE
Air Transport

AKZO NOBEL DECORATIVE CAMBODIA (ANDCC)
Commerce

ALCATEL TRADE INTERNATIONAL (ATI)
Telecommunications

ANGKOR VILLAGE
Hotel

ART STUDIO
Architecture

ARTE CAMBODIA
Architecture

ASIA FLOUR MILL CORPORATION (AFMC)
Mill

ASIAN TRAILS LTD.
Tourism

AWS CAMBODIA
BAYON HOTEL
Hotel

BIO-RAD
BONS VOYAGES
Tourism

BOUYGUES DRAGAGES
Construction/public works

CABINET DE KINESITHERAPIE
Physiotherapy

CAMBODGE NOUVEAU
Journalism

CAMBODIA AIRPORT MANAGEMENT SERVICES (CAMS)
Aéronautique

CAMBODIA MANAGEMENT CONSULT
Consultancy

CAMBODIA ENGINEERING CONSULTANTS (CEC)
Consultancy

CAP
Painting, sealing and electricity

CELLIERS D'ASIE (LES)
Wines and spirits

CERCLE BLEU (LE)
Architecture and town planning

CHRUN ENTREPRISES
Representation of civil engineers

CMA CONSTRUCTION MANAGEMENT
Construction

CMC COMPTOIR MEDICAL DU CAMBODGE
Pharmaceuticals

COCHIN ARCHITECTS CO.LTD
Architecture

COMIN KHMERE CO LTD
Imports and electrical goods

COMPAGNIE FRANCAISE DE COMMERCE S.A.R.L. (CFC)
Trade, judicial advice and accounting

COULEURS D'ASIE

CREDIT AGRICOLE INDOSUEZ
Banking

CYS CONSTRUCTION LTD
Construction

DANZAS AEI INTERNATIONAL (CAMBODGE) LTD
Transport and storage

DBD ELECTRICITE
Electrical installation

DG DISTRIBUTION
News agency, distribution of french publications

DUMEZ - GTM CAMBODGE
BTP

ECO MULTI SERVICE (EMS)

EDITION DU MEKONG (CAMBODGE SOIR)
Edition

ELECTRICITE DE FRANCEc/o EDC
Electrical distribution

EMBASSY PLACE
Apartment blocks

ETDE

EUROP CONTINENTS SARL
Medical equipment, packaging

EXODIS CO.LTD

FINANCIERE DU CAMBODGE
Construction

FINE SKY INVESTMENT LTD

FRANASIE IMPORT EXPORT LTD

FREMICAM

GATEC Ingenierie
Engineering

GEODIS OVERSEAS CO

GIDE LOYRETTE NOUEL

GOLDEN GARDEN PRODUCE CO. LTD

GRAPHIC ROOTS
Graphic publications

GROUPE 117 (G-117)
Architecture

GSC GENERAL SERVICE CAMBODGE

HUNG HIEP (CAMBODIA) CO. LTD
Automobiles

HYPHENS MARKETING AND TECHNICAL
SERVICES CAMBODIA
Industrial pharmaceuticals, medical and hospital equipment

INCAMKO INVESTMENT CO. LTD

INCHCAPE c/o ARMSTRONG ENGINEERING

INDOCHINE INSURANCE
Insurance

INDOCHINE INSURANCE UNION
Insurance

INNOV

INTERQUESS CO LTD
Yellow pages

JEAN DESJOYAUX CAMBODIA CO. LTD
Swimming pools

KAK & ASSOCIES

KC MKK CO. LTD

KHMER CONTRACTOR & IMPORT EXPORT CO. LTD
Paper, printing, cosmetic products

KHMER EMERGENCY SERVICES

KHMER VILLAGE

KOSAN ENGINEERING

KOYODA

LBL INTERNATIONAL
Construction

LCT ARCHITECTURE
Cabinet of architecture and town planning

M & B ENTERPRISE CO., LTD

M & M PRODUCTS

MAESTRIA CAMBODIA CO. LTD

MANITEL

MEDIA BUSINESS NETWORK (MBN)

MEDICO TRADING
Pharmaceuticals

MEDICOM

MEKONG ISLAND
Tourism and parks

MEWAS

MOET HENNESSY ASIA PTE. LTD
Alcohol

NAGA MEDICAL CENTER PHNOM PENH c/o
Hospital

NAGA PHARMACY CENTER c/o
Pharmaceuticals

NARITA MEDICAL IMPORT EXPORT

Import/Export of pharmaceutical products

NARITA TRANSPORT
Transit et Transport

ORIENT- LA CHINE CO. LTD

PHOENIX IMPORT EXPORT AND TRANSPORTATION
Distribution, trade and transport

POCHENTONG AIRPORT CONSTRUCTION JV
(PAC JV LTD)

PONLOEU KOMAR CO. LTD
Aluminium

PPM PHARMA PRODUCT MANUFACTURING
Production of pharmaceutical products

PRODISTRI c/o

PROTEK CAMBODIA SECURITY CO. LTD
Security

PYRAMIDE

RITEXIM
Lubricants

RM ASIA CO. LTD
Mechanical and electrical engineering

ROUSSEL CAMBODGE
Import of pharmaceutical products

SADE Branch Office

SAFEGE c/o
Engineering and water distribution

SDV CAMBODGE
Storage and transport

SEITA CAMBODGE c/o
Tobacco and cigarettes

SERVIER INTERNATIONAL

SIKA SERVICE

SOCIETE CONCESSIONNAIRE DE L'AEROPORT (SCA)
Airport businesses

SOFITEL ROYAL ANGKOR
Hotel

STV CONSULTANTS

SUNGATE CO. LTD

THAI HUOT TRADING
Import and distribution of health products

TOTAL CAMBODGE c/o
Distribution and petroleum products

VICHAR TOUR
Tour operations and tourism

VILLA PARC

YVES ROCHER
Cosmetics

German Enterprises

SIEMENS AG REP. CAMBODIA
Telecommunications

Hong Kong Enterprises

ASIA INSURANCE
Insurance

GENNON GARMENT MFG LTD
Garments

HECHTER (CAMBODIA) GARMENT LTD
Garments

PAK SHUN KNITTING FACTORY CO. LTD
Knitting

SUN WAH FISHERIES CO. LTD
Seafood-processing

TACK FAT GARMENT CAMBODIA LTD
Garments

YGM MTD
Garments

Korean Enterprises

DA JOO CAMBODIA LTD
Garments

SAM HAN CAMBODIA FABRIC CO. LTD
Garments

Macao Enterprises

M&V INTERNATIONAL MANUFACTURING LTD
Garments

Malaysian Enterprises

CAM PAPER INDUSTRIES LTD
Paper products

CAMBODIA UTILITIES PVT LTD
Electricity Generation

CAMBREW LTD
Beer and soft drink

JUNE TEXTILES CO. LTD
Garments

PCCS GARMENT LTD
Garments

Dutch Enterprises

SHELL COMPANY OF CAMBODIA LTD
Petroleum distribution

Portuguese Enterprises

FRANCO KNITTING GARMENT FACTORY LTD.
Knitting

Singaporean Enterprises

CAMBODIA BEVERAGE COMPANY (COCA-COLA)
Soft Drinks

CAMBODIA CARTONS LIMITED
Corrugated cartons & other of packaging materials

HOTELCAMBODIANA
Hotel

HOTEL LE ROYAL
Hotel

MCC TRANSPORT SINGAPORE PTE. LTD
Shipping, Transport

MICASA HOTEL
Hotel

"SBC-SINGAPORE BANKING CORPORATION LTD"
Banking

SUNTEX PTE LTD
Garments

Swiss Enterprises

DIETHELM TRAVEL
Travel and Tours

KUEHNE & NAGEL (CAMBODIA)
Logistics

NESTLE DAIRY (CAMBODIA) LTD
Food and beverage products

SGS CAMBODIA LIAISON OFFICE
Customs inspection services

Taïwanese Enterprises

KING FIRST INDUSTRIAL CO. LTD
Garments

ROO HSING GARMENT CO. LTD
Garments

TAI YANG ENTERPRISES CO. LTD
Garments

VICTORY LONG AGE CAMBODIA LTD.
Footwear

Thai Enterprises

PRESIDENT FOODS (CAMBODIA) CO. LTD
Instant noodles

United States Enterprises

CALTEX CAMBODIA LIMITED
Petroleum distribution and marketing

DFDL
Legal and Tax advisors

KPMG
Accounting, taxation, auditing services

MANHATTAN TEXTILE AND GARMENT CORP.
Garments & textiles

TILLEKE & GIBBINS AND ASSOCIATES
Legal services

Multi Origin Enterprises

Cambodia - China

CAMBODIA PHARMACEUTICAL ENTERPRISE
Medical products

Cambodia - Indonesia

CAMINTEL
Telecommunications

Cambodia - France - Malaysia

SCA (SOCIETE CONCESSIONNAIRE DE L'AEROPORT)
Phnom Penh and Siem Reap International Airports Concession

Cambodia - Japan

EASTERN STEEL INDUSTRY CORP
Galvanised iron sheets

KHAOU CHULY MKK CO. LTD
Concrete & asphalt products

Cambodia - Malaysia

MUHIBBAH ENGINEERING (CAMBODIA) CO. LTD
Construction engineering

Sources: French enterprises 2002/2003, Cambodian Embassy in Paris.
Main enterprises in Cambodia, UNCTAD.

SUNWAY HOTEL PHNOM PENH
Hotel

Cambodia - Singapore

CAMBODIA BREWERY LTD
Beer and softdrink

Cambodia - Singapore - United Kingdom

BRITISH AMERICAN TOBACCO (BAT)
Cigarettes

Cambodia - Taiwan

Q.M.I. INDUSTRIAL CO. LTD
Garments

Cambodia - Thailand

CAMBODIA SAMART COMMUNICATION
Telecommunications

CCB- CAMBODIA COMMERCIAL BANK LTD
Banking

Cambodia - Thailand - China - Hong Kong

ASIA INSURANCE
Insurance

Cambodia - United States

CPL CAMBODIA PROPETIES LTD
Property management

JUPITER POWER ASIA CO. LTD
Power Plant

Malaysia - Thailand

CAMBODIA SAMART COMMUNICATION
Telecommunications

Hong Kong - Portugal - Australia

SHOE PREMIER (CAMBODIA) CO. LTD
Footwear

ANNEX 5b – Main investors in Cambodia

S.N	Name of company	Country of ownership	Business	Contact details
1.	Asia Insurance Mr. Pascal Brandt-Gagnon General Manager	Hong Kong, China, Thailand and Cambodia	Insurance	No. 91 Norodom Blvd, Phnom Penh Tel: 855 23 – 427 981 H/p: 855 12 – 812 090 Fax: 855 23 – 216 969 E-mail: gmo@asiainsurance.com.kh
2.	British American Tobacco Cambodia (BAT) Mr. John Nelson General Manager	United Kingdom, Singapore and Cambodia	Cigarettes	No. 1121 National Road 2, Phnom Penh Tel: 855 23 – 430 011/360 691 H/p: 855 12 – 773 355 Fax: 855 23 – 360 692 E-mail: john_nelson@bat.com
3.	Caltex Cambodia Limited Mr. Edgar C. Mondigo Acting General Manager	United States	Petroleum distribution and marketing	Olympic Motor Building, 173 Nehru Boulevard, Phnom Penh Tel: 855 23 – 880 570/3 H/p: 855 12 – 803 852 Fax: 855 23 – 880 691 E-mail: caltex@bigpond.com.kh
4.	Cam Paper Industries LTD Mr. Wong Ing Yong General Manager	Malaysia	Paper product	Phum Russey, Sangkat StungMeanChey, Phnom Penh Tel: 855 23 – 368 969 Fax: 855 23 – 368 969 E-mail: cam.paper@online.com.kh
5.	Cambodia Beverage Company (Coca-Cola) Ms. Denise Lauwens General Manager	Singapore	Soft drinks	No. 278 Road National 5, Khum Russey Keo, Phnom Penh Tel: 855 23 – 428 995/6 Fax: 855 23 – 428 992 E-mail: dlauwens@apac.ko.com
6.	Cambodia Brewery Ltd Mr. Koh Tai Hong General Manager	Singapore and Cambodia	Beer and soft drink	Village Robos Angkagne, District, Kien Svay, Kandal Province Tel: 855 23 – 722 683 M/p: 855 12 – 888 898 Fax: 855 23 – 723 104 E-mail: taihong.koh@cbl.com.kh
7.	Cambodia Cartons Limited Mr. Seah Chye Ping General Manager	Singaporean	Corrugated cartons & other of packaging materials	National Road No 4, Phum DomNak Ampil, Khum Domnak Ampil, Srock angsnoul, Kandal Province Tel: 855 23 – 369 088 M/p: 855 12 – 809 088 Fax: 855 23 - 369 083 E-mail: cclcartons@bigpond.com.kh
8.	Cambodia Haining Group Co., Ltd. Mr. Xiao Wen Hui Office Supervisor	China	Agriculture - Castor	# 20, Street 47, Phnom Penh Tel: 855 23 - 428 068 855 12 - 837 618 Fax: 855 23 - 428 068 E-mail: haining@bigpond.com.kh

9.	Cambodia Mekong Bank Public Limited Mr. Khov Boun Chhay President&CEO	Cambodian	Banking service	1 Kramuon Sar St, Khan Daun Penh, Phnom Penh, Cambodia Tel: 855 23 – 217 112/424 980 Fax: 855 23 –217 122/424 326 DID:855 23 – 424 323 Direct Fax: 855 23 – 424 990 E-mail: khov.bc@mekongbank.com
10.	Cambodia Pharmaceutical Enterprise Mrs. Wong Swie Hwa General Manager	China/ Cambodia	Medical production	#36 Geordimitrov, Sangkat Mittapheap,Khan 7 Makara, Phnom Penh Tel: 855 23 – 880 112/880 496 Fax: 855 23 – 880 296 E-mail: cpe@online.com.kh
11.	Cambodia Samart Communication Mr. Somchai Lertwiset-Theerakul Chief Executive Officer	Malaysia and Thailand	Telecom-munications	#56, Preah Norodom Boulevard, Sangkat Chhey Chomneas, Khan Daun Penh, Phnom Penh Tel: 855 16 – 810 001/3 Fax: 855 16 – 810 006 Website: hello016-gsm.com/
12.	Cambodia Utilities Pvt, Ltd. Mr. Lim Teow Hin General manager	Malaysia	Electricity generation	National Road No.2, Chhey Sankat Chak Ang Re, Khan Mean, Phnom Penh Tel: 855 23 – 425 592 Fax: 855 23 – 425 050 E-mail: limth@cupl.com.kh
13.	Cambrew Ltd. Mr. Teh Sing Chief Operating Officer	Malaysia	Beer and softdrink	No. 215 Norodom Boulevard, Sangkat Tonle Bassac, Khan Chamcarmon, Phnom Penh Tel: 855 23 – 987 663 H/p: 855 16 – 888 028 Fax: 855 23 – 360 668 E-mail: tehsing@online.com.kh cambrew@online.com.kh
14.	CamGSM/Mobitel Mr. David Spriggs General Manager	Cambodia	Telecom-munications	No. 33, Sihanouk Boulevard, Phnom Penh Tel: 855 12 – 800 800 855 12 – 812 812 Fax: 855 23 – 801 801 E-mail: david.spriggs@camgsm.com.kh
15.	CAMINCO Mr. Vong Sandap General Director	Cambodia	General insurance services	# 28, Corner St. Preah Ang Eng & St. Moh Kosamak, Phnom Penh Tel: 855 23 - 722 043 855 11 - 777 507 855 12 - 792 277 Fax: 855 23 – 427 810 E-mail: caminco@camnet.com.kh
16.	Camintel Mr. Nhek Kosal Vythyea Managing Director	Cambodia and Indonesia	Telecom-munications	No. 1 Corner of Terak Vithei Preah Sisowath and Vithei Phsar Dek, Phnom Penh Tel: 855 23 – 981 234 / 986 789 Fax: 855 23 – 981 277 E-mail: sales@camnintel.com
17.	Canadia Bank Ltd. Cambodia Mr. Pong Khea Se General Manager	Cambodia	Banking	No. 265-269, Ang Duong (St. 110), Phnom Penh Tel: 855 23 – 215 286 855 23 – 215 087 Fax: 855 23 – 427 064 E-mail: canadia@camnet.com.kh Telex: CANADIA KA36188 Swift code: CADIKHPP

18.	CCB- Cambodia Commercial Bank Ltd. Mr. Sahasin Yuttarat General Manager	Thailand and Cambodia	Banking	No. 26, Monivong Blvd, Phnom Penh Tel: 855 23 – 426 145 / 213 601 855 23 – 213 602 Fax: 855 23 – 426 116 E-mail: ccbpp@online.com.kh Website: www.ccb-cambodia.com/ Swift code: SICOKHPP
19.	CPL Cambodia Properties Ltd Mr. Cheng Kheng Managing Director	Cambodia and United States	Property management	#219, St. 19, Sangkat Chhey ChomNeas, Khan Daun Penh, Phnom Penh Tel: 855 23 – 213 666 / 855 11 – 811 333 855 12 – 804 255 Fax: 855 23 – 363 315 E-mail: cplpnp@online.com.kh
20.	Da Joo Cambodia Ltd Mr. Robert Hwang General Manager	Korea	Garments	Phom Angkeo, Khum Kantork, Srok Angsoul, Kandal Province. Tel: 855 12 – 900 323 Fax: 855 23 – 219 605 E-mail: robert@dajoointernational.com
21.	DFDL Mr. L-Martin Desautels Managing Director	United States	Legal and tax advisers	No. 45, Preah Suramarith Boulevard, Phnom Penh Tel: 855 23 – 210 400 855 12 – 805 552 Fax: 855 23 – 428 227 E-mail: info@dfdl.com.kh Website: www.dfdl.com.kh
22.	Diethelm Travel Mr. Pierre Jungo General Manager	Switzerland	Travel and tours	No. 65, Street 240, Phnom Penh Tel: 855 23 – 219 151 Fax: 855 23 – 219 150 E-mail: dtc@dtc.com.kh
23.	Eastern Steel Industry Corp Oknha Kong Triv President	Japan and Cambodia	Galvanized iron sheets	No. 1157, National Road No.2, Chak Angre Leu, Srok Meanchhey, Phnom Penh Tel: 855 23 – 721 880 Fax: 855 23 – 425 037 E-mail: tairaku@online.com.kh
24.	Franco Knitting Garment Factory Ltd. Mr. Cheong Chi Hou Director	Portugal	Knitting	Phum Kav, Khum Beikchan, Srok Ang Snoul, Kandal Province, Tel: 855 23 – 223 368 / 361 839 Fax: 855 23 – 216 633 E-mail: franco@bigpond.com.kh
25.	Gennon Garment MFG Ltd Mr. Jacky Y.K. Mau General Manager	Hong Kong	Garments	Phum Chong Thnol, Khum Tek Thlar, Russey Keo District, Phnom Penh Tel: 855 23 – 368 388 / 368 389 Fax: 855 23 – 368 398 E-mail: gennon_cbd@online.com.kh
26.	Hechter (Cambodia) Garment Ltd Mr. Wong Sing Tun General Manager	Hong Kong	Garments	No 15,Works Canadia industrial Park, Phnom Penh. Tel: 855 23 – 985 633 Fax: 855 23 – 985 693 E-mail: hechtergarment@every.com.kh

27.	Hotel Cambodiana Mr. Michel Horn Managing Director	Singapore	Hotel	313 Sisowath Quay, Phnom Penh Tel: 855 23 – 426 288 855 23 – 218 189 Fax: 855 23 – 426 290/426 392 E-mail: luxury@hotelcambodiana.com.kh marketing@hotelcambodiana.com.kh Website: www.hotelcambodiana.com

28.	Hotel Intercontinental
	Phnom Penh
	Mr. Edwin Bucher
	General Manager
		Cambodia	Hotel	No. 296
				Mao Tse Tong Boulevard,
				Phnom Penh
				Tel: 855 23 – 424 888
				   855 16 – 924 888
				Fax: 855 23 – 424 910
				E-mail: edwin_bucher@interconti.com
				   phnompenh@interconti.com

29.	Hotel Le Royal Mr. Stephan Gnaegi General Manager	Singapore	Hotel	# 92, Phnom Penh Tel: 855 23 – 981 888 855 12 – 931 271 Fax: 855 23 – 981 168 E-mail: emailus.leroyal@raffles.com
30.	Indochina Research Limited Mr. Tim Smyth Managing Director	Australia	Marketing research & consultant services	No. 9 Mao Tse Tung Boulevard, Phnom Penh Tel: 855 23 – 215 184 / 362 753 855 12 – 810 594 Fax: 855 23 – 215 190 E-mail: tsmyth@irl.com.kh
31.	Indochine Insurance Mr. Philippe Lenain Managing Director	France	Insurance	No. 55 Street 178, Phnom Penh Tel: 855 23 – 210 622 855 12 – 821 320 Fax: 855 23 – 210 501 E-mail: plenain@indochine.com.kh Website: www.indochine.net
32.	June Textiles Co., Ltd Mr. Lee Thai Khit Managing Director	Malaysia	Garments	Russian Boulevard, Borei 100 Khnong, Sankat Tek Thla, Khan Russey Keo, Phnom Penh Tel: 855 23 – 365 288 / 883 338 H/p: 855 12 – 833 338 Fax: 855 23 – 363 398 /881 238 E-mail: junetex@camnet.com.kh tklee@everyday.com.kh
33.	Jupiter Power Asia Co., Ltd Mr. Sok Seila President	Cambodian & United States	Power plant	#777Eo, Kampuchea Krom Blvd, Phnom Penh Tel: 855 23 – 884 777/881 891 Fax: 855 23 – 881 892 E-mail: JUPITER@online.com.kh
34.	Khaou Chuly MKK Co., Ltd Mr. Khaou Chuly President	Japan and Cambodia	Concrete & asphalt products	# 15, Street 306, Sangkat Boeung Keng Kang, Khan chamcarmon, Phnom Penh Tel: 855 23 – 218 080/218 082 Fax: 855 23 – 2170 36 POBox 942 E-mail: kcd@online.com.kh
35.	King First Industrial Co., Ltd Mr. Thomas Lo General Manager	Taiwan	Garments	B Seat, Group 3, Road 15, Sangkat Toul Sang ker, Khan Russey Keo, Phnom Penh. Tel: 855 23 – 725 791 855 12 – 932 166 Fax: 855 23 – 723 266 / 890 310 E-mail: king1st@online.com.kh

36.	Kong Hong Garment Co., Ltd Oknha Sok Hong Managing Director	Cambodia	Garments	No 474, Monivong Blvd, Sangkat Tonle Bassac, Khan chamcarmon, Phnom Penh. Tel: 855 23 – 212 796 855 16 – 866 666 Fax: 855 23 – 218 472 E-mail: konghong_shp@online.com.kh
37.	KPMG Mr. David King Director	United States	Accounting, taxation, auditing services	No. 2 Street 208, Phnom Penh Tel: 855 23 –216 899 Fax: 855 23 – 216 405 / 217 279 E-mail: kpmg@bigpond.com.kh
38.	Kuehne & Nagel (Cambodia) Mr. Ngin Monidera General Manager	Switzerland	Logistics	Olympic Motor Bldg, 173 Nehru Boulevard Tel: 855 23 – 881 654 / 884 875/6 855 12 – 820 205 Fax: 855 23 – 881 656 E-mail: ngin.monidera@kuehne-nagel.com
39.	M&V International Manufacturing Ltd. Mr. Thomas Keong Managing Director	Macao	Garments	#754, Sangkat Chak Angre Krom, Khan Meanchhey, Phnom Penh. Tel: 855 23 – 425 043 / 425 041/425 010 Fax: 855 23 – 425 001 E-mail: info_camb@mvintl.com
40.	Manhattan Textile and Garment Corp. Mr. Larry Kao General Manager	United States	Garments and textile	# 62, Street 348, Sangkat Toul Svay Prey II, Khan Chamkarmon, Phnom Penh. Tel: 855 23 – 721 000 855 12 – 903 399 Fax: 855 23 – 721 198 E-mail: larrykao@medtecs.com.kh
41.	MCC Transport Singapore Pte. Ltd. Mr. Preben Hartvig Andersen Senior owner's representative	Singapore	Shipping, transport	No. 26, Hotel Cambodiana, Phnom Penh Tel: 855 23 – 216 744 / 216 745 Fax: 855 23 – 217 843 / 213 843 E-mail: pnhmtsmng@mc.com.sg
42.	Micasa Hotel Mr. Mike Lee General Manager	Singapore	Hotel	# 313, Sisowath Quay, Phnom Penh Tel: 855 23 – 214 555 Fax: 855 23 – 213 071 / 217 111 E-mail: reservation@micasa.com.kh Website: www.cambodia.micasahotel.com
43.	Mighti-Spectra knitting Factory Co., Ltd Mr. Wong Man Sang Director	British	Knitting	National Road No 6A, Phum Bakheng Khum Prelab, Srok Russey Keo, Phnom Penh Tel: 855 23 - 219 666 Fax: 855 23 – 219 658 E-mail: mighti@bigpond.com.kh
44.	Mong Reththy Investment Cambodia Oil Palm Co., Ltd. Oknha Mong Reththy General Director	Cambodia	Palm oil plantation	No 152S, Preah Norodom Boulevard, Phnom Penh, Cambodia Tel: 855 23 – 211 065 / 211 117 Fax: 855 23 – 216 496 E-mail: mrtgroup@bigpond.com.kh Website http://www.mongreththy.com

45.	Muhibbah Engineering (Cambodia) Co. Ltd Okhna Khieng Hann Senior Director	Cambodia and Malaysia	Construction engineering	# 315, Mao Tse Tung Boulevard, Phnom Penh Tel: 855 23 – 367 988 / 883 366 Fax: 855 23 – 366 888 E-mail: mec@muhibbah.com.kh Website: www.muhibbah.com
46.	Nestlé Dairy (Cambodia) Ltd Mr. Bertrand J. Sigwalt General Manager	Switzerland	Food and beverage products	# 1748, Road National 5, Phnom Penh Tel: 855 23 – 430 180/ 1 855 12 – 820 720 Fax: 855 23 – 430 171 E-mail: Bertrand.Sigwalt@nestle.com.kh
47.	Pak Shun Knitting Factory Co., Ltd Mrs. Sam Yu General Manager	Hong Kong	Knitting	National Road No 2, Sangkat ChakAng Re Krom, Khan Mean Chey, Phnom Penh Tel: 855 23 – 425 688 / 366 366 Fax: 855 23 - 425 000 / 363 515 E-mail: pakshun@online.com.kh
48.	PCCS Garment Ltd Mr. Tan Keat Chong General Manager	Malaysia	Garments	Federation of Russia Boulevard, Sangkat Tek Thla, Khan Russey Keo, Phnom Penh Tel: 855 23 – 882 138/982 422 855 12 – 908 168 Fax: 855 23 – 982 477 E-mail: pccsgl@bigpond.com.kh kctan@pccsgroup.net
49.	President Foods (Cambodia) Co., Ltd Okhna Kong Triv Mr. Su Chai Ratanajiajaroen Director	Thailand	Instant noodle	Phum Mor, Road Chamkar Doung, Sangkat Dangkor, Phnom Penh, Tel: 855 23 – 363 987 Fax: 855 23 – 364 688 E-mail: N/A
50.	Q.M.I. Industrial Co., Ltd Mr. Kong Sang General Manager	Cambodia and Taiwan	Garments	Phum Trapang Pout, Sangkat Chom Chao, Khan Dangkor, Phnom Pehn. Tel: 855 12 – 829 888 Fax: 855 23 – 890 309 / 890 310 E-mail: qmi_daisy@online.com.kh
51.	Roo Hsing Garment Co. Ltd Mr. Kan Chin Chen Manager	Taiwan	Garments	New Road, Sangkat Toul Sangke, Khan Russey Keo, Phnom Penh. Tel: 855 23 – 430 152 855 23 – 367 701/2 Fax: 855 23 – 430 153 E-mail: jackychen@rooshing.com
52.	Sabrina Garment Manufacturing Corp. Mr. Steed Cheung General Manager	China	Garments	Phum Trapeang Russey, Khum Sambo, Srok SamrongTong, Kompong Speu. Tel: 855 23 – 367 785/6 855 16 – 991 209 Fax: 855 12 – 844 420 E-mail: sabrina@mobitel.com.kh
53.	Sam Han Cambodia Fabric Co., Ltd. Mr. Kim Do Sam President	Korea	Knitting	#68Eo, Phum Toul Sang Ke, Sangkat Toul Sang Ke, Khan Russey Keo, Phnom Penh. Tel: 855 23 - 368 287 Fax: 855 23 – 368 297 E-mail: samhan@everyday.com.kh

54.	SBC- Singapore Banking Corporation Ltd Mr. Kun Swee Tiong Andy Chief Executive Officer	Singapore	Banking	No. 68, Samdech Pan (St.214), Phnom Penh Tel: 855 23 – 217 771/2 217 737/377 Fax: 855 23 – 212 121 E-mail: info@sbc-bank.com Website: www.sbc-bank.com
55.	SCA (Société Concessionnaire de l'Aéroport) Mr. Bruno Blanc-Fontenille General Manager	France, Malaysia and Cambodia	Phnom Penh and Siem Reap International Airports Concession	Phnom Penh International Airport P.O.Box 1256, Phnom Penh Tel: 855 23 – 890 022 855 23 – 890 523/4 Fax: 855 23 – 890 395 E-mail: bruno.blanc-fontenille@sca.com.kh Website: www.cambodia-airports.com/
56.	SGS Cambodia Liaison Office Mr. Malcolm Reid Managing Director	Switzerland	Customs inspection services	No. 368, E0 Street 163, Chamkarmon, Olympic, Phnom Penh Tel: 855 23 – 210 730 to 210 736 Fax: 855 23 – 210 737 E-mail: sgs.cambodia_lo@sgs.com
57.	Shandong Demian group (Cambodia) Textile Co., Ltd. Mr. Zhou Rong Shui General Manager	China	Textile	# 168, Street 41, Sangkat 1, Khan Mittapeap, Sihanouk ville Tel: 855 23 – 884 806 855 34 – 939 650 Fax: 855 34 – 939 652 E-mail: rongsh-3@163.com
58.	Shell Company of Cambodia Ltd Mr. Nestor Tan Country Manager	Netherlands	Petroleum distribution	# 216, Norodom Boulevard, Sangkat Tonle Bassac, Khan Chamcarmon, Phnom Penh Tel: 855 23 – 215 180 855 12 – 813 228 Fax: 855 23 – 215 170 P.O.Box 49 E-mail: nestor.tan@shell.com.kh
59.	Shoe premier (Cambodia) Co., Ltd Mr. Zheng Xian Jiang General Manager	Hong kong, Portugal and Australia	Footwear	Phum Toul Sang Ke, Sangkat Toul Sang Ke, Khan Russey Keo, Phnom Penh Tel: 855 23 – 982 212 Fax: 855 23 – 982 313 E-mail: shoepremier@bigpond.com.kh
60.	Siemens AG Rep. Cambodia Mr. Wolfgang Kitz Managing Director	Germany	Telecommunication	1st Floor, # 15, Street 214, Sangkat Boeung Reang, Khan Daun Penh, Phnom Penh Tel: 855 23 – 216 990 M/p: 855 12 – 806 777 Fax: 855 23 – 216 991 E-mail: siemens.cambodia@siemens.com.kh
61.	Su Tong Fang Group Ying Kan Garment Mr. Qiang Chun General Manager	China	Garments	C Seat, Group 3, Road 15, Sangkat Toul Sang Ke, Khan Russey Keo Phnom Penh. Tel: 855 23 - 723 188 Fax: 855 23 – 365 508 E-mail: chinaqiangchun@sohu.com textiles@bigpond.com.kh

62.	Sun Wah fisheries Co., Ltd Mr. Gilbert Manager	Hong Kong / China	Seafood-processing	No. 196Eo, St. 63, Group 56, Sangkat Boeung KengKang I, Khan Chamcarmon, Phnom Penh Tel: 855 23 - 361 628 - Phnom Penh 855 34 - 320 089- Sihanouk Ville Fax: 855 34 - 320 083 E-mail: 012809988@mobitel.com.kh
63.	Suntex Pte Ltd Mr. Chen Wai Pan General Manager	Singapore	Garments	No. 8, Street Veng Sreng, Khan Daungkor, Phnom Penh Tel: 855 23 – 424 778 / 985 688 Fax: 855 23 – 424 777 / 424 799 E-mail: suntexat@online.com.kh wilson@oceanskyintl.com
64.	Sunway Hotel Phnom Penh Mr. Manfred Hager General Manager	Malaysia and Cambodia	Hotel	# 1, Street 92, Phnom Penh Tel: 855 23 – 430 333 Fax: 855 23 – 430 339 E-mail: gm.sunway.pnh@bigpond.com.kh
65.	Tack Fat Garment Cambodia Ltd Mr. Fransis So Managing Director	Hong Kong	Garments	#1159, National Road No 2, Chak Angre Leu, Khan Meanchhey, Phnom Penh Tel: 855 23 – 367 888 / 300 682 / 300 650 / 300 681 Fax: 855 23 – 362 828 E-mail: francis@tackfat.com.kh tfcam@bigpond.com.kh
66.	Tai Yang Enterprises Co., Ltd Ms. Kiki Wang Director	Taiwan	Garments	National Road No 4, Phum BekChan, Khum BekChan, Srok Ang Snoul, Kandal Province. Tel: 855 23 – 367 897 855 23 - 367 894/5 Fax: 855 23 –367 897 E-mail: kiki@tai-nan.tw
67.	Tilleke & Gibbins and Associates Mr. Brett Sciaroni President Partner	United States	Law firm	No. 56 Sothearos Boulevard, Phnom Penh Tel: 855 23 – 362 670 855 12 – 802 274 Fax: 855 23 – 362 671 E-mail: zirconium@bigpond.com.kh tga@bigpond.com.kh
68.	TOTAL Cambodge Mr. Alexander Kislandski General Manager	France	Petroleum distribution	2nd FI, Hong Kong Centre, Phnom Penh Tel: 855 23 – 218 630 855 12 - 813 454 Fax: 855 23 - 217 662 E-mail: alexandre.Kislanski@total.com.kh
69.	TTY Co., Ltd Mrs. Seng Touch General Manager	Cambodia	Crumb rubber, tapioca mill, granite and saw mill	Sihanouk Boulevard, # 97E1, Sangkat Chaktomouk, Khan Daun Penh, Phnom Penh Tel: 855 23 – 214 513 H/p: 855 12 – 801 313 Fax: 855 23 – 214 513 E-mail: memot@camnet.com.kh
70.	Universal Apparel (Cambodia) Co.,Ltd Mr. Lin Zhi Yuan General Manager	China	Garments	Veng Sreng Street, Phum Treang Thlong Sangkat Chom Chao, Srok Dangkor, Phnom Penh Tel: 855 23 – 802 266/802 277 Fax: 855 23 – 985 612 E-mail: universal@camnet.com.kh

71.	Victory Long Age Cambodia Ltd. Mr. Tsen Wen Pin General Manager	Taiwan	Footwear	New Road, Sangkat Kakab, Khan DangKor, Phnom Penh Tel: 855 23 – 890 077 Fax: 855 23 - 890 055 E-mail: longage@online.com.kh
72.	Wing Tai Apparel (Cambodia) Ltd Mr. Wan Kwok Ming General Manager	British	Garments	National Road No 5, Phum Samaki, Khum Russey Keo, Srok Russey Keo, Phnom Penh. Tel: 855 23 – 428 534 / 428 669 Fax: 855 23 – 368 199 E-mail: alanwan@online.com.kh
73.	YGM Ltd Ms.K.Y. Ling General Manager	Hong Kong	Garments	National Road No 4, Phum Tek Thlar, Sangkat Tek Thlar, Khan Russey Keo, Phnom Penh, Tel: 855 23 – 883 183 855 12 – 980 168 Fax: 855 23 – 890 393 E-mail: ky.ling@ygm.com.hk

ANNEX 6 – Cambodia at a Glance

Data	Figures
Population	13,124,764
Median age	*Total:* 19.2 years
Life expectancy at birth	*Total population:* 57.92 years *Male:* 55.49 years *Female:* 60.47 years
HIV/AIDS – people living with HIV/AIDS	170,000
Ethnic groups	Khmer 90%, Vietnamese 5%, Chinese 1%, other 4%
Languages	Khmer (official) 95%, French, English
Literacy	*Definition:* age 15 and over can read and write *Total population:* 69.9%
Land use	*Arable land:* 20.96% *Permanent crops:* 0.61% *Other:* 78.43% (1998 est. including forest 45%)
Area comparative	Twice Portugal or half Germany
Climate	Tropical; rainy, monsoon season (May to November); dry season (December to April); little seasonal temperature variation
Evaluation extremes	*Lowest point:* Gulf of Thailand 0 m *Highest point:* Phnum Aoral 1,810 m
Natural Resources	Timber, gemstones, some iron ore, manganese, phosphates, hydropower potential, oil &gas potential
Economy overview	Since 1999, the first full year of peace in 30 years, progress was made on economic reforms and growth resumed at 5.0%. In 2004, the long-term development suffers of the lacks education and productive skills, and from an almost total lack of basic infrastructure. Projects are scheduled to compensate these economic brakes.
GDP	3 billions $ (at market price, 2002 current $)
Population below poverty line	36% (1997 est.)
Inflation rate (consumer prices)	3.8% (2001) 3.3% (2002 est.)
Unemployment rate	2.8% (1999 est.)

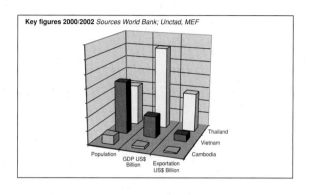

Key figures 2000/2002 *Sources World Bank; Unctad, MEF*

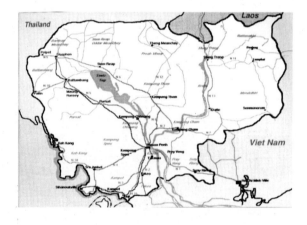

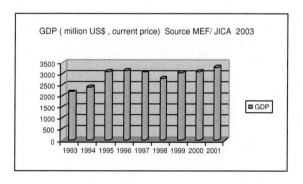

GDP (million US$, current price) Source MEF/ JICA 2003

Industries	Tourism, garments, shoes, agro processing (rice milling, fishing)
Electricity production by source	*Fossil fuel:* 65% *Hydro:* 35%
Electricity – consumption	110.6 million kWh (2001)
Agriculture products	Rice, rubber, fruit, vegetables, fish

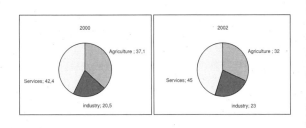

Exports	$1.77 billion FOB (2002 est.)
Exports products	Garments, shoes, rubber, rice, fish
Exports partners	US 61.5%, Germany 9.0%, UK 7.2%, Singapore 4.5%, Japan 3.8% (2002)
Imports	$2.3 billion FOB. (2002 est.)
Imports – commodities	Petroleum products, cigarettes, gold, construction materials, machinery, motors vehicles
Imports - partners	Thailand 30.2%, Singapore 21.5%, Hong Kong 10.2%, China 7.8%, Vietnam 6.6%, Taiwan 4.7% (2002)
Debt – external	$829 million (1999 est.)

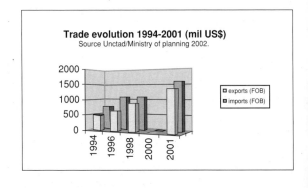

Currency	Riel (KHR)

Telephones – main lines in use	65,000 (2003)
Telephones – mobile cellular	80,000 (2000) / 650 000 (2003)
Telephone system	*General assessment:* adequate landline and/or cellular service in Phnom Penh and other provincial cities; rural areas have little telephone service *International:* adequate but expensive landline and cellular service available to all countries from Phnom Penh and major provincial cities.
Radio broadcast stations	AM 7, FM 3 short ware 3 (1999)
Television broadcast stations	6 (2003)
Internet country code	.kh
Internet Service Providers (ISPs)	2 (2000) – 7 (2003)
Internet users	10,000 (2002)

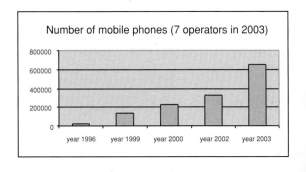

Railways	*Total:* 602 km *Narrow gauge:* 602 km 1.000-m gauge (2002)
Roads	*Total:* 35,769 km *Paved:* 4,165 km *Unpaved:* 31,604 km (1997)
Waterways	3,700 km
Ports and harbors	Sihanoukville, Phnom Penh
Airports	2 international airports (Phnom Penh & Siem Reap) – 2 heliports 21 in total (2002) – 5 with paved runway - 16 unpaved

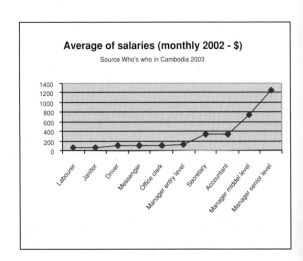

Government type	Multiparty democracy under a constitutional monarchy established in September 1993
Capital	Phnom Penh
Constitution	Promulgated 21 September 1993
Legal system	Primarily a civil law mixture of French-influenced codes from the United Nation. Transitional Authority in Cambodia (UNTAC) period.
Juridical branch	Supreme Council of the Magistracy (provided for in the constitution and formed in December 1997); Supreme Court (and lower courts) exercises judicial authority.
Main Political parties and leaders	– Cambodia People's Party or CPP [CHEA SIM]; – Cooperative Cambodia or FUNCINPEC [Prince NORODOM RANARIDDH]; – Sam Rangsi Party or SRP (formerly Khmer Nation Party or KNP) [SAM RANGSI]

WTO	Cambodia admitted to WTO in September 2003 in Cancun; pending ratification by National Assembly
ASEAN	The association is composed of 10 countries: Brunei, Cambodia, Indonesia, Lao PDR, Malaysia, Myanmar, Philippines, Singapore, Thailand, Viet Nam
REGIONAL AGREEMENT	Thailand, Myanmar Lao and Cambodia declared in Bangkok in August 2003 a Strategy for economic cooperation (despite of economic sanctions announced by USA).

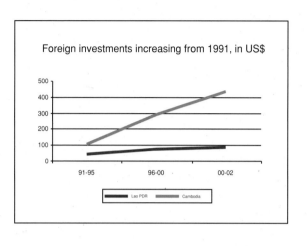

Foreign investments increasing from 1991, in US$

European Commission

New Business Opportunities for EU Companies in Cambodia – An Investor's Guidebook

Luxembourg: Office for Official Publications of the European Communities

2005 — xvii, 79 pp. — 21 x 29.7 cm

ISBN 92-894-7527-7